✳✳✳

Growing Up in the 1850s

❋❋❋❋❋❋❋❋❋❋❋❋❋❋❋❋❋❋❋❋❋❋❋❋❋❋❋❋❋❋❋❋❋❋❋❋

Growing Up in the 1850s

The Journal of Agnes Lee

Edited by Mary Custis Lee deButts

Published for the

Robert E. Lee Memorial Association, Inc.

by The University of North Carolina Press

Chapel Hill and London

Manufactured in the United States of America

97   11   10   9

Library of Congress Cataloging in Publication Data

Lee, Agnes, 1841–1873
Growing up in the 1850s

Includes index.
1. Lee, Robert E. (Robert Edward), 1807–1870—Family.
2. Lee, Agnes, 1841–1873. 3. Lee family. 4. Children—
United States—Biography. I. deButts, Mary Custis Lee.
II. Title.
E467.1.L4L37   1984   973.6′092′2   84-10452
ISBN 0-8078-1622-1
ISBN 0-8078-4243-5 (pbk.)

FRONTISPIECE

*Eleanor Agnes Lee. This picture was taken later than the dates of the journal,
but it is the earliest one available.
Courtesy of Mrs. W. Hunter deButts.*

Contents

vi
Contents

Illustrations

Foreword

The journal of Agnes Lee came to me many years ago from my father, Robert E. Lee, Jr., who was the younger brother Rob mentioned in its pages. In the same notebook, though written later, were the recollections by Mildred Lee, Agnes' sister, as well as some photographs and newspaper clippings. Once or twice I made halfhearted attempts to have these published but it was not until January of 1983 that my thoughts became serious. A rather ominous remark made by my cousin, Mrs. Walter Williams—"It is later than we think"—caused me to lend her the journal and it is largely due to her quiet persistence and interest that I finally started this project. It was she who suggested that I consult Mr. Paul Nagel, Director of the Virginia Historical Society and author of several books. His help and enthusiasm along with the resources of the Society have been invaluable, and when this little book sees the light of day, it will be because of him. Valued assistance came also from Mr. Howson Cole of the Society's staff. Mrs. Leslie Cheek, Director for Virginia of the Robert E. Lee Memorial Association, deserves a large share of thanks for securing the Association's important financial aid and for her helpful contributions, especially her "Brief Historical Note." Many people cooperated in finding photographs and drawings suitable to the period. These include the staffs of Arlington House, the United States

Military Academy Library, Stuart Hall, and Washington and Lee University. My grandson, Robert E. L. deButts, Jr., wrote the introduction, a present-day evaluation from three generations down, and spent long hours searching for identities for "Cousin C——" or "Mrs. T——" in order to complete his very helpful annotations. The index, that time-consuming and necessary final note, is entirely due to the kindness and effort of Mrs. Paul Nagel—my sincere thanks go to her.

Except for the omission of some repetitious passages, the journal is published as it was written with its spelling and punctuation intact. Scholars desirous of consulting the journal as a whole may see it at the library of the Virginia Historical Society in Richmond.

The journal has been broken into five sections or chapters determined by Agnes' residence at the time, but it will be obvious to the reader that while in one place, Agnes reminisces about another, and that Arlington, her much loved home, comes into all the chapters. Part Two includes recollections by the youngest of the Lee sisters, Mildred, describing Agnes' death and revealing a similar love for Arlington. Part Three contains letters between Agnes and her parents.

While at the Virginia Female Institute Agnes wrote, "O my journal I hope no eyes will see you save mine, they only will excuse my follies & my weaknesses." Today, one hundred and thirty years later, on thinking over our present-day follies and weaknesses, I feel the time is suitable for other eyes to see the journal, and I believe that the recollections of Mildred Lee cast a revealing light on these glimpses of the Lees' family life.

Mary Custis Lee deButts
"Nordley," January 1984

A Brief Historical Note

Arlington House, the scene of much of Agnes Lee's journal, is one of our nation's treasures, not only because of its powerful architecture, but because it unites the memories of two of America's greatest families.

Agnes' father, Robert E. Lee, the most beloved figure in the history of the South, was himself a hero worshiper. His idol was George Washington. When Lee married Mary Anne Randolph Custis in June 1831 at Arlington, he came as close as possible to becoming a member of the Washington family, since Mary's father, George Washington Parke Custis, grandson of Martha Washington, was the adopted son of George.

George Washington Parke Custis, a remarkable but little remembered man, was the creator of this equally remarkable house. After the death of his grandmother, Martha Custis Washington, in 1802, the twenty-one-year-old George moved from Mt. Vernon to his own land a few miles up the river to the north. The site he selected for his house is one of the finest in Virginia, at the fall line of the Potomac, where two-hundred-foot palisades rise on the south bank to command a sweeping view of the city of Washington.

The deepest passion of George W. P. Custis' life was keeping alive the memory of his adoptive grandfather. When the furnishings of Mt. Vernon were put up for sale after Martha's death, young George used most of his available funds to purchase objects that had surrounded his namesake. He therefore had to proceed slowly on the construction of his new house as money and materials came in from the 15,000 acres of his other rented farms.

Although there was a persistent tradition that William Thornton may have had a hand in the early design of Arlington, it is now believed to be the work of George Hadfield, the second architect of the Capitol. Building began in 1803 on the north wing that was then called Mt. Washington; in it were stored the Washington memorabilia. The south wing was completed in 1804 and George moved his bride into what must have been a most inconvenient combination of rooms in two separate houses. The name was then changed to Arlington after the Custis ancestral house on the Eastern Shore. Insufficient funds and the War of 1812 delayed the construction of the central block, but it was finished at last in 1818. The massive Greek Revival portico dominating the high bluff is visible for miles; it remains one of the most striking landmarks of Washington.

George W. P. Custis was a dilettante, an enthusiast with many interests and not inconsiderable talents. He was an amateur painter, playwright, orator, and collector. A man neither tall nor handsome, his exuberance and inexhaustible hospitality attracted people of all ages and stations. The abundant ease in which he lived was due to his wisdom in choosing his wife, Mary Lee Fitzhugh of Ravensworth, in Fairfax County, not far from Washington. This loving, capable young woman managed the large house and staff of slaves with affectionate efficiency. She was a born gardener, and the beauty that she developed in her husband's "park" was an abiding source of pleasure to her family and friends, as Agnes' journal testifies. Best of all, she created a home life that was happy and fostering; it was in this richly nourishing atmosphere that her only surviving child and namesake, Mary Anne Randolph Custis, grew to maturity, and in which her Lee grandchildren fortunately shared.

Mary Anne Custis looked like her father. She was small, artistic, and inherited his love of friends and relatives. Since her mother was a distant cousin of Robert Edward Lee, she had known him and his brothers and sisters from childhood. How long Robert had loved her no one knows, but they were married at Arlington on 30 June 1831, two years after young Lieutenant Lee had graduated second in his class from West Point.

For the first three years of their life together they lived at Fortress Monroe, Virginia, Lee's second post. In November 1834 they were ordered to Washington and began to look for a small house for themselves and their two-year-old son, Custis, named for his grandfather. Nothing suitable could be found, and they were invited to stay on at Arlington. Although in the following years they moved in and out as Lee's duties demanded, it remained the place they loved and called home until the hostilities of 1861 closed it to them forever.

No matter where he was stationed, Robert Lee managed if it were humanly possible to come home to Arlington for Christmas with his growing family. Although Mrs. Lee was never robust and was in ill health most of her life, she produced seven children in rapid succession. Lee felt sure of being introduced to a new one every Christmas; to be with them and to play with them were antidotes to every stress. He was always homesick for them. "If I could only," he wrote Mrs. Lee from St. Louis, "get a squeeze at that little fellow turning up his sweet mouth to 'Keese babe!'"

The second locale of the journal is West Point, where Lee was superintendent of the United States Military Academy from September 1852 to 31 March 1855. The beauty of the situation of "The Point" on the bluffs overlooking the Hudson must have been doubly congenial to the older members of the family. It was not unlike that of Arlington and it was also the location of Fort Clinton; the house that had been Washington's headquarters during the Revolutionary War stood just to the north. The Academy had been enlarged and much improved since Lee's cadet years, and the superintendent's house was comfortable and attractive. The reader will enjoy Agnes' changing view of West Point as she grows from child to young girl.

Staunton, Virginia, where Agnes was a student, was a town of 5,000 when she and her sister Anne enrolled at "Staunton Jail," as she calls the Virginia Female Institute, in 1856. Situated in the Valley of Virginia in idyllic surroundings of mountains, meadows, and rivers, the town itself made little impression on the homesick schoolgirl. It can be seen more clearly through her father's eyes, only five years later, during the Valley Campaign, as he rode away from Staunton. He wrote his wife: ". . . I passed over [a part of the road] in the summer of 1840, on my return from St. Louis, after bringing you home. If anyone had then told me that the next time I traveled that road would have been on my present errand, I should have supposed him insane. I enjoyed the mountains as I rode along. The views are magnificent—the valleys so beautiful, the scenery so peaceful. What a glorious world Almighty God has given us. How thankless and ungrateful we are, and how we labour to mar his gifts."

One final word must be said about the intellectual climate in which the Lee children were reared. Their grandfather Custis stipulated in his will that his slaves be freed, and their grandmother had devoted much time and effort not only to instructing them in the Christian faith that was so large a part of her life, but also teaching them to read and write in preparation for a life of independence. It will be remembered that Liberia was founded by the American Colonization Society in 1822 and became an independent republic in 1847. As executor of his father-in-law's will, Robert Edward Lee carried out Mr. Custis' provisions. He freed

A Brief Historical Note

the last of the slaves in 1862 during the war, but those who wished to settle in Liberia were sent before hostilities broke out. Letters from some of the Liberians telling Lee of their new lives slipped through the Federal naval blockade. The three generations at Arlington were not blinded by privilege to the prejudices of their time. Although the young Lees were never wealthy, theirs was a rich heritage.

Mary Tyler Freeman Cheek

Introduction

Eleanor Agnes Lee was the fifth child of Robert Edward Lee and his wife, Mary Anne Randolph Custis. She was born at Arlington in 1841 and died thirty-two years later at Lexington.

Agnes began her journal in December 1852 at the insistence of a governess employed for Agnes and her sister Anne; she made the last entry five years later, at the beginning of 1858. Agnes' journal documents quite an interesting five years in the life of an equally interesting young woman. It is offered here in the belief that Agnes' account of a girlhood in antebellum America is valuable in its own right. The changes of the Civil War lay in the future when Agnes made the final entry in her journal. During the time she wrote, her father was promoted to lieutenant colonel in the 2nd Cavalry, and when she mentioned him, it was usually to regret his absence.

Although as a military family the Lees often moved from post to post, they always thought of Arlington as home. Agnes' love for the place was evident throughout her journal, whether she was living at West Point, where her father was superintendent of the Military Academy, or at Staunton, where she went to school. Arlington was built by George Washington Parke Custis, Agnes' maternal grandfather, who had made the house into something of a museum; visitors could view Washington's silver and china, his library, and

Arlington as sketched by Benson J. Lossing in 1853. Though they moved to various places as their father's profession required, the Lee children always considered Arlington their home.
Courtesy of the Arlington House Collection.

other memorabilia. Custis was also a minor literary figure, having written several plays on American themes. As a result, the number of visitors was large even for a Virginia home of the period; Agnes mentions several of her grandfather's guests, including President Pierce and Washington Irving.

Both of Agnes' residences when she was away from Arlington

were schools, but it would be difficult to find two schools more different than the U.S. Military Academy and the Virginia Female Institute. Agnes' status varied strikingly from one to the other, as did her perception of that status. Arriving at West Point when she was twelve, Agnes complained of adults and college-aged cadets "... treating children as grown persons," pushing her into a role she was not sure she wanted. Once accustomed to West Point, however, such a role came easier; before she left she was surprised to find herself referring to cadets as boys. Her girls' school must have been an unwelcome change from the Academy, for she lamented being "... only an *insignificant* school girl," and reminisced on her days at "that enchanting spot."

A strong current of religious belief runs throughout the journal. Although Agnes seems to have been a regular and attentive churchgoer, her decision to be confirmed was not lightly made; she often questioned her own worthiness and gave her religion a great deal of thought. The passages that deal with her religious beliefs and with the deaths of Mr. and Mrs. Custis are among the few in which Agnes seems to open up and express her thoughts freely. Religion also becomes increasingly central in the more mature passages toward the end of the journal.

Alongside Agnes' religious beliefs run a familiarity with and sentimentality toward death that may seem curious to modern readers. We would expect comment on the death of a grandparent, but Agnes was also interested in the deaths of cousins, pets, cadets, servants, and acquaintances. Columbus' death made more of an impression on her than did anything else in Irving's four-volume work. A Good Friday evokes more comment than several Christmases; a visit to a family graveyard is more interesting than either. This emphasis may merely result from the introspective mood in which one is most likely to make a journal entry, but it also indicates an important difference between our way of looking at the world and that of nineteenth-century Americans.

Virginius C. Hall of the Virginia Historical Society writes: "Sorrow for the dead loomed large in the minds and hearts of our nineteenth century forebears. It was a lachrymose time, a time in which grief was not only a sentiment to cherish and brood over in solitude, as Washington Irving noted, but to adopt as a companion when one ventured forth in the world again."

Several of Agnes' other journal entries are also worthy of note. She twice mentions teaching the Custis slave children, showing that the laws prohibiting such teaching were ignored by her father, a man not wont to disobey authority. She also comments on a honeymoon trip taken by two servants. Agnes indicates her strong aversion to tobacco use and passes along a good-natured jab at men, the "lords of creation."

"It will be amusing in later years to know what I did and felt when I was young," wrote Agnes as she began her journal. Today it can do more than merely amuse; Agnes Lee has provided us with a valuable account of girlhood in the 1850s.

Robert Edward Lee deButts, Jr.

✳✳✳✳✳✳✳✳✳✳✳✳✳✳✳✳✳✳✳✳✳✳✳✳✳✳✳✳✳✳✳✳✳✳✳

Part One
The Journal of Agnes Lee

Arlington

Christmas eve December 24th 1852.

I am flying about preparing presents and hanging up stockings. I am in a perfect twirl can't keep still a minute. Tomorrow is Christmas. O what a happy time I expect to have. I have received most of my gifts already viz. a new dress from Grandpa[1] which I am going to put on tomorrow morning. "Angel over the right shoulder" from Grandma.[2] "The distant hills" from Cousin M. Goldsborough.[3] A portmonaie from Miss Susan Poor[4] (our governess). Cousin Mary Meade is my only dependance. How I wish they all were here then my cup of happiness would be full. But never mind next summer we will all meet. I do so long for next summer for many reasons and visiting West Point is one of the principle.

1. Granpa—Agnes' maternal grandfather, George Washington Parke Custis (1781–1857). A grandson of Martha Washington, Custis and his sister Nelly were adopted by George Washington after the death of their father, John Parke Custis (1753–1781).
2. Grandma—Mary Lee (Fitzhugh) Custis (1788–1853).
3. Cousin M. Goldsborough—probably Mary Goldsborough, a cousin of Mrs. Lee.
4. Susan Poor—Agnes and her sister Anne were staying at Arlington with their grandparents while the rest of the family was at West Point, where Lee had recently been appointed superintendent of the U.S. Military Academy, or away at school. Mrs. Lee had hired a governess in the hope of "stirring them up a little."

I will miss Aunt Lewis'[5] Christmas present so much she always gave me something. I shall value her gifts more now since I may receive no more of them. She died last July. She has gone to her reward for she died full of trust in her Savior. Death is so dreadful to the wicked but delightful to the righteous.

Miss Sue says I must keep a journal it will improve my "style". At any rate it will be amusing in after years to know what I did and felt when I was young!

Jan. 1st 1853.

The New Year! how quickly time flies. It seems but yesterday that we hailed "52".

I hope with the New Year I will commence my studies resolved to improve my understanding by gaining useful knowledge.

I must describe the Christmas holidays. Well twenty mins. before five Manda[6] rushed in and caught me "Christmas gift."

I was up in an instant, examined my stocking, dressed ran upstairs and caught them all there. I spent the whole morning giving and receiving gifts and being as happy as possible. It rained hard all day so we could not go to church.

5th.

There has been much company coming and going during the holidays so I have not been able to practise much. Today is bright and beautiful. I am so glad, we are so tired of rainy weather. My

5. Aunt Lewis—Eleanor (Nelly) Parke (Custis) Lewis (1779–1852), Agnes' namesake, one of G. W. P. Custis' sisters.

6. Manda, no doubt, was a daughter of one of the house servants. To catch someone Christmas gift was an old custom in Virginia, and is still observed in some homes. The earliest riser steals quietly to a sleeper and calls "Christmas gift!" and in theory the person caught must give the catcher a present.

*George Washington Parke Custis, descendant of Martha Washington and
owner of Arlington—the grandpa of Agnes' journal.
In the collection of the Corcoran Gallery of Art.*

Christmas holidays seem to have been much wasted. I can preserve no system when there is so much company. When I am at school it is a different matter then I am obliged to perform my duties.

12th.

Today Cousin Lum[7] dropped her scissors and they stuck in the floor, which is said to be the sign some one is coming and true enough soon afterwards William and Mary Gurley with a friend and his bride paid us a visit.

Having had chills I did not come down. I have just received a letter from Rooney.[8] He says when he is sick he has to take Castor-oil. I have to swallow pills. I dislike both very much but of the two, pills I think are preferable.

19th.

Half of Jan. has passed. I can't believe it, time flies so rapidly. We are watching with great anxiety the ice on the river for fear of losing it before our ice house is filled.

Last Saturday we spent a day at Mrs. Packard's. We had a large company, consisting of six girls. Nimmie and Genny Fairfax, Nanny P., Annie[9] and myself. Cousin M. Meade went with us to the

7. Cousin Lum—probably Columbia Williams, a first cousin of Mrs. Lee.
8. Rooney—William Henry Fitzhugh Lee (1837–1891), Agnes' brother. Rooney later enrolled at Harvard University after failing to gain an appointment to the U.S. Military Academy. He dropped out of Harvard when he received a commission in the U.S. Army. During the Civil War he became a major general in the Confederate Army.
9. Annie—Anne Carter Lee (1839–1862), one of Agnes' sisters.

Seminary building[10] to see the matron. We had a very pleasant day, read aloud, played Dominoes, ran down the road and amused ourselves in various ways. We returned home quite tired after our day's pleasure and found Cousin Lum in the midst of ironing muslins for a visit to Chantilly.[11]

Feb. 2nd.

Last Sat. Annie and I drove down to the ferry and walked over to Georgetown to see Mrs. Stevenson's baby and little Custis Usphur.[12] Grandma was sick but as we had written we were coming she thought we had better go. Last Saturday week Washy Stuart skated out here on the canal. Laura[13] was staying with us. We four took a long walk down to the spring, rock, ice-house and all about. Grandpa's ice-house is quite full. So now we care not whether it freezes or does not freeze for ourselves. But I am not so uncharatable as to be indifferent as to whether other persons fill their houses. Sunday Grandma, for a wonder, Annie and I went to church.

Daniel[14] was sent to town today. When he came in I *felt* there was a letter for me, but Grandpa put the bag down and went on with his dinner, Grandma insisted on having it opened and how great was my delight when I saw "Miss Agnes Lee", upon an envelope containing three letters, from Papa, from Mamma and

10. Seminary Building—the Virginia Theological Seminary, located outside the city of Alexandria.
11. Chantilly—Fairfax county home of Mrs. Calvert Stuart, an aunt of Mrs. Lee.
12. Custis Usphur—Custis Upshur, a second cousin of Agnes, son of Admiral and Kate Williams Upshur.
13. Washy and Laura Stuart—cousins of Agnes, possibly granddaughters of Calvert Stuart.
14. Daniel—the coachman at Arlington.

Mary Lee Fitzhugh Custis, mistress of Arlington and Agnes' grandma.
Courtesy of the Virginia Historical Society.

from Rob.[15] Miss Sue, who has been in Washington, returned about eleven with Major Wheeler.

Feb. 16th.

Last Thursday I was walking in my garden at recess when I saw two crocuses. I almost thought it was Spring they looked so bright and beautiful with their little heads turned towards the sun as if drinking in his warm beams. That was the *tenth* of Feb. I was so proud that *my* flowers should bloom before any others. We did not go to church Sunday. About 12 o'clock Mr. Stark, Mr. Stuart and Cousin John Calvert[16] came over for an hour or two. Monday we expected Washington Irving and Mr. Lanman[17] and prepared accordingly but they did not come until next day. I merely had a peep at Mr. Irving. I wish he had dined as we expected, then I should have seen more of him.

23rd.

Last Sunday we heard a remarkably good sermon from Mr. Dana.[18] "O woman great is thy faith, be it unto thee even as thou wilt." (Mat.XV.28). Every one remarked how good it was. In the evening I had my little *dark* scholars though they were loth to tare themselves from their sleigh riding.

15. Rob—Robert Edward Lee, Jr. (1843–1914), Agnes' brother. A student at the University of Virginia when the war broke out, he enlisted in the Rockbridge Artillery as a private and later was brevetted captain in the cavalry. He was the author of *Recollections and Letters of General Lee* (1904).
16. Cousin John Calvert—a cousin of Mrs. Lee.
17. Mr. Lanman—Charles Lanman. For an account of Irving's visit to Arlington, see Lanman's "A Day With Washington Irving," *National Intelligencer*, 23 March 1857.
18. Mr. Dana—Charles Dana. Dana was pastor of Christ Church, Alexandria, and a friend of the Lee family.

I shall now describe my "22nd." Annie said she could not go—so I went alone and spent the day at Dr. Fairfax's.[19] We saw the procession several times, of the Militia, and engines, very prettily dressed, with little boys standing upon the latter arrayed most fancifully. Then we went to "Liberty Hall" to hear the oration. If I *could* have heard, I should have been better pleased. Mr. Danforth read, first, a chapt. in the Bible; I heard it was in Deuteronomy, and also the name of God occasionally, then he prayed a long time, and when he had finished was "clapped"! Mr. Meade read the "Farewell address" for which he was "clapped" several times. Mr. Beach was the orator, what I did hear seemed to be very fine and he was applauded at least fifty times though not ten in the room knew whether it was Latin, Greek, or German! Then all called for "Custis"; Grandpa came forward, made a polite bow. I was so tired or I should like to have listened as his was not long, but I could not. I counted almost a hundred times they "Clapped" and finding they never would stop applauding I stopped counting. But I can't write more now—

16th Wed.

I have not written for two weeks on account of sickness. Grandpa and Miss Sue went to the Inauguration[20] through all of the snow. Grandpa never has missed one. Mrs. Sigourney[21] has sent Grandma "Examples of Life & Death," Grandpa, "The faded Hope." He gave his to me, it is beautiful. Monday we went to the schoolroom though Miss S. had not returned, presently I heard so much noise

19. Dr. Fairfax—Orlando Fairfax of Alexandria, also a friend of the family.
20. The Inauguration—of Franklin Pierce.
21. Mrs. Sigourney—Lydia Sigourney (1791–1856). Mrs. Sigourney, author of many moral and educational works written primarily for young women, had been a friend of Mr. Custis' since 1833, when she helped him attract attention to the need for a monument to mark the grave of Mary Washington.

downstairs we concluded she had arrived but found instead a gentleman to see Arlington & its wonders. Mr. Lossing[22] shortly made his appearance and then Miss Sue, had had a miserable time crossing—and a "glorious fourth." It is very cold, I fear all of our violets & johnquills will be killed. I do so long to work in *my* garden but as soon as I commence it freezes.

23rd.

Mr. & Mrs. Lossing with their daughter arrived yesterday. Cora is ten, and I am sure she is small enough to be seven. Mr. Burton paid us a second visit a few days ago. Miss S—— has asked him during his previous one to bring her a picture of Arlington. As he did not produce it this time Grandma mentioned it. "Oh" said he, "I searched all over W—— but could not find the peculiar crayons I work in." Grandma said then you might do it in New York & send it, "O no! the crayon would rub off but I'll certainly do it." I venture to say we will never see that picture. Surely the Capital of the *U.S.* might furnish *crayons.*

Apr. 6th.

It is a delightful day, quite a treat after so much rain. Everything is so springlike. The fruit trees are blooming beautifully. I fear we will miss all of the fruit here we go to West Point so early but as Brother[23] says there is a great deal in the "Superintendant's" garden, we can enjoy that. Sat. morning Cousin Em. & I took a walk in the woods to gather moss & wild flowers. I found the first

22. Mr. Lossing—Benson John Lossing (1813–1891).
23. Brother—George Washington Custis Lee (1832–1913), Agnes' oldest brother. Custis was at this time a cadet at West Point; he later became a major general in the Confederate Army and, after his father's death, president of Washington and Lee University.

"Forget me not." They are such dear little flowers. I have a hen "Brunetta" with nine little chickens, & another fine pullet Aunt Stella[24] has just presented me called Eudora. She is very wild yet.

13th.

Miss Sue's brother has been spending a few days here. They are expected from W—— today with some Mr. & Mrs. Peters,[25] time will show which.

20th.

Alderman Peters, Mrs. Cook & her baby they proved to be. Mrs. C's baby is the sweetest & best I almost ever saw. His name is Arthur Peters Custis Cook, more than he can carry I fear. Orton[26] (for he is getting too big to be called Bunny now) walked in while I was practising. In fact were I to attempt to write down each arrival I would have a task; so many distinguished guests must not feel slighted if they are left out in this record. The everyday life of a little school girl of twelve years is not startling. And my thoughts, they say you ought to put your thoughts in a journal—but I cannot.

May 4th.

Two weeks have passed since I last wrote, what months & years they have been. I do not yet realize what has happened. My dar-

24. Aunt Stella—probably an Arlington servant.
25. Some Mr. and Mrs. Peters—the Peters family lived in Georgetown and were cousins of Mrs. Lee.
26. Orton—William Orton Williams, a first cousin of Mrs. Lee. After the deaths of his parents he was raised by his sister Markie; both were very close to the Lees. Orton later wanted to marry Agnes but her father, although fond of Orton, apparently withheld his consent, thinking him too reckless. He was captured behind Union lines and hanged as a spy in 1863.

ling Grandmamma has passed away from this earth. O I *can't* believe it! I know it is true. But it seems like a dream—O I wish I could wake! To see her only once more. How lonely it is to feel you haven't a Grandma any more. I know she died a Christian & to think she is with our Savior in Heaven. They tell me we must not wish her back but this is the first person I loved that has been ever taken from me, & it will seem so hard. Poor Grandpa is almost heart broken & is quite sick. I wish I could write connectedly on the subject. O it seems almost too sacred even to write about. But I will try. Thursday evening (21st April) we drove in to Alexandria with Mrs. Cook, Grandma had a headache then, but we supposed it was one of her usual attacks. The Doctor was sent for next morning. He apprehended no danger but would return next day. Sat. morning he looked very grave & told us she was in much peril—but I could not believe it. Mama was written & telegraphed for, we asked her if she had any messages, but her mind wandered a little & she made no answer. She clasped us in her arms & murmured some affectionate words for her little grandchildren. I climbed on the bed by her, I saw her breath come more & more slowly, she murmured the Lord's prayer—with that on her lips she died! That was twenty minutes after one. I gazed on her perfectly bewildered my eyes wildly asked for one more sign of life. It was so impossible to believe she was *dead*! Aunt Peter[27] arrived shortly beforehand. The servants stood around weeping for their unconscious mistress. My headache distracted me & poor Grandpa, I can hardly think of his agony. He knelt by her bedside, & implored God to spare her or to make him submissive to His will. I went to my own trundle bed & wished for Mamma. She did not arrive until a day or two afterwards. We followed my Grandma's remains to the grave on Wed. 27th. Grandma was just sixty five the day before her death. O that funeral, it seemed as if we could not let her be shut up in the dark earth. Though I know it was only her

27. Aunt Peter—Mary Parke (Custis) Peter (1777–1854), Mr. Custis' sister.

body, her angel spirit may have been hovering above us, wanting to comfort her poor children. It is so beautiful to look through the green trees at the blue sky above & think she may be there.

May 11th.

Everything on earth is looking so bright & beautiful today. Grandpa is recovering slowly & I am sure when he can walk out the fine air will revive him. I have been working in my garden. O how Grandma enjoyed her garden! I loved it dearly before but now I love it more. When I look at her favorite flowers they remind me so of her. She has gone to a land where the flowers are far more beautiful. May we all meet her there! Mamma has received many letters from sympathizing friends, I know many many will feel deeply what this house has lost.

May 25th.

The bridge is mended, what a comfort. We have two months before vacation, I must say I am not sorry. But when it comes, I don't know what I'll do, where I'll go or anything. All of my delightful anticipations of West Point have gone now. I am almost tempted to murmur against God for calling Grandmamma away when it seemed impossible to spare her, but she would not come to earth again after having tasted the joys of Heaven.

June 1st.

Grandpa is recovering rapidly. I am so glad, he is going to take a drive today. The time is approaching for vacation. I do not like to think of leaving Arlington now. I love it more than ever. If we do go I hope it is only for a little while, this is always *my home.* And such a beautiful one, I am sure I ought to love it. I am so glad Grandma's remains are here for I can visit them whenever I want to. I love to carry flowers & place them on her grave, then sit down by it & think of her beyond the blue sky, I almost fancy I see her looking down through the tall trees. O I try to do as I know she would like me to do!

June 15th.

It is warm. Mamma says she is going to W. P. early in July. I don't want to go except for a little while & not then if Grandpa don't go, I cant bear the idea of leaving him all alone. Vacation will be welcome, I almost go asleep over my lessons, but then West Point & not to know when I may come back to Arlington! Charlie & Louis Conrad came out in an omnibus yesterday with Nora, bringing us two dear little english rabbits, a white & a grey.

June 22nd.

Grandpa says "he will *try* to take the journey by the middle of July if he is well enough". I am glad except it will delay our vacation. I would like to visit W.P., I want to take the journey, see the place, hear the music. I think my mump of motion is largely developed but I don't want to stay there & I am afraid I'll have to, however we can't do everything in this world we "want to", so I must not think my lot harder than others.

Pres. Pearce & his wife drove over here yesterday, their carriage was very handsome.

The moon is so beautiful every night I do love to look at it, everything is so peaceful so enchanting. O how beautiful this world is, would it were as good as lovely!

Wed. 29th.

We received a long letter from Fitzhugh[28] as I am trying to call him. It was the most interesting I have ever had from him, he had visited the Hipodrome & found it a "complete humbug" he says. Both Fitz's & Sister's[29] vacation will soon commence, how happy we would all be together if there was only *one* more.

July 6th.

Papa, Rob. & Mil.[30] are coming this evening, I am so glad, I am ready to jump. I don't know where exactly, but I can't help thinking of them. They will be so glad to see us. I suppose they have grown very much. I know how the buns will delight them, & doubtless they will be charmed with Tom.[31] We went to the school house Sunday & saw the sacrament administered, it was very impressive.

July 13th.

Miss Sue has gone, I wonder when I shall see her again. O I felt *so* sad when we parted!—there is only one gain, it may be of benefit to my journal; it is so impossible to write unrestrainedly when you feel some one is going to look over what you have just written. Pa & the children did not come until Thursday. Our meeting was mournful the new comers felt there was one missing who used to give them a happy greeting. Sister & Fitzhugh are coming next Saturday. How pleasant to be all together, except Brother poor fellow he can't leave West Point.

28. Fitzhugh—Rooney.
29. Sister—Mary Custis Lee (1835–1918), Agnes' oldest sister.
30. Mil.—Mildred Childe Lee (1846–1905), another of Agnes' sisters.
31. Tom—a cat.

Robert E. Lee, Jr.   *Mildred Childe Lee*

*The two youngest children of Robert E. Lee. These pictures show them at
their approximate ages just before the journal begins.
Courtesy of Mrs. W. Hunter deButts.*

Two pencil sketches by Robert E. Lee of soldiers in the Mexican Army. They were probably done during the Mexican War (1846–48) and sent home to

20th.

Sister & Fitz. arrived Sat. the former was not very well. Fitz—— is perfectly enormous & just the same. Sunday eve. we went into church & heard Bishop Johns[32] preach, I don't think I ever heard such a sermon before. I was almost breathless. The text was "& Simon Peter answered him, Lord to whom shall we go? thou hast the words of eternal life." I remember almost every word of it! It was an invitation to come to Christ. I solemnly determined to dedicate myself to God & I have tried, but Oh! I don't think I have improved in the least there is so much to try me. I do wish I was a christian! but it is so hard to be one. After the sermon Papa, Annie

32. Bishop Johns—John Johns (1796–1876), Episcopal Bishop of Virginia.

his children. They were found in a scrap book kept by his daughters.
Courtesy of Mrs. W. Hunter deButts.

& Mary were confirmed. I wish A—— & I could have been confirmed together. They have promised to be Christians. May they
have strength given them to keep their vows.

25th.

I have been quite sick for two or three days. Aunt Maria,[33] Cousin
Mary Goldsborough came out to spend a day & the two latter
remained until Thursday. During my invalidism I committed to
memory a poem by Gray called "The Bard." It has nine long verses
but is beautiful.

33. Aunt Maria—Anna Maria Sarah (Goldsborough) Fitzhugh (1796–1874), Mrs.
Lee's aunt.

Aug. 6th.

We returned yesterday from Ravensworth.[34] Last Wed. evening Pa, Ma, Rob & I started for R—— arrived about six. Rob & I immediately set out for the rock & ran all over the garden. The pangs of hunger assailed us sorely on our return but we were soon gratified by a most excellent supper. The next morning after rising from breakfast table at *nine* we bent our steps towards the lake regaled ourselves with a few peaches on the way to the horror of some little colored children on the hill who stared at us as if we were wild beasts. In the evening we went to the grave-yard where my beloved Grandma's father & mother and only brother are burried, also Aunt Anne's[35] first child & one or two other persons I believe. After climbing to the top of the high wall which surrounds it & which with the trees near are covered with poison-oak, we obtained a view of the scene inside. There was a stone monument in the centre erected to the memory of my great uncle William & two near the wall just like the former side by side of *her parents.*[36] Courageous as I usually am I confess I felt something like fear or rather awe steal over me as I sat on that mouldy wall surrounded by dark cedars & other trees, the poisonous vines waving over & around me & looking down upon that mass of rank & poisonous weeds while my thoughts sank to those who rested beneath the tombs. I stole away saddened and subdued. It is so solemn to realize the presence of Death. Oh may I be prepared to meet him. However Rob soon rouzed me by a challenge to climb a portion of the rock he had. I succeeded & then we amused ourselves by playing all over it. We next went to a cherry tree not far distant & espying some gum Rob (after trying in vain to climb the tree by

34. Ravensworth—Fairfax County home of Mrs. A. M. Fitzhugh (Aunt Maria).
35. Aunt Anne—Anne Randolph Fitzhugh, Mrs. Custis' sister.
36. Her parents—William Fitzhugh (1741–1809) and Anne (Randolph) Fitzhugh (1747?–1805), Mrs. Custis' parents.

means of a bean pole we had with some difficulty procured) commenced to break off the gum with the pole's sharp point in the end we obtained quite a pretty collection.

Friday morn. we both felt badly so after breakfast we went to our rooms, made ourselves very comfortable on the bed, Rob. soon fell asleep while I read. That evening we returned home after such a nice little visit to sweet old Ravensworth but I am so tired writing I must stop.

8th.

I have this morning determined to have two hours to myself daily for writing & study I am now standing at the toilet journalizing. I have read the Introduction & one chapter in "Abbott's young Christians, translated a French fable, & read a chap. in Pinnocks Goldsmith's England. Intend to do more tomorrow, besides today I mean to practice an hour, read the "animated Nature, a chap. in Mrs. S——'s letters & sew or knit.

It is decided we must leave for West Point in a week. How can I say farewell to Arlington! How can I quit this dear place never *never* perhaps to return. It is heart rending but I suppose I must bear it.

Friday 26th.

I really ought to be ashamed of myself for not having written before, but the longer I have put it off the harder it has been to begin. But where am I? Really at West Point but not the West Point of my imagination. I am so homesick. I long for Arlington my precious Arlington my own dear *home*, but I will acknowledge any other place by that title. O how I love my home—thou art an old & tried friend; as for this place I know nothing about it. And my precious Grandma's grave! I wonder who places flowers there now—the flowers *she* loved, who takes away the weeds & sticks now. O it almost breaks my heart it makes me cry. I must not talk so, I must try and be contented but next summer is so long to wait. I shall try & quietly recall the past & give a connected account of what has happened since Aug. 8th.

Well about a week before we started on our long journey Annie & I paid a farewell visit to Laura. had a very pleasent time & "oceans" of peaches. We returned Friday eve. to commence our preparations for Tuesday. That day came alas! too quickly. In the morning I walked to Grandma's grave & placed my last [ ] there. I kissed the mound o'er & o'er but the cold earth returned not my affection so I walked sadly away. We had to leave our bunnys sweet little things it was very hard but we feared the journey would kill them. Boon made a pen for them in the north western corner of the vegetable garden. So Tuesday afternoon I went to tell them goodbye. I hugged & kissed them but little did they appreciate my affection or my sadness. We were soon whirling in the express train to Balt. where we spent several days. Aunt Anne[37] is so sweet & good I love her so much. I promised to write to her & really must but we have been so busy these few days. Eliza is the only house servant we have had so we have arranged the rooms, set the table, been waiters, cooks, & a little of everything, quite *Northern* already. But our cook arrived yesterday the waiter will tomorrow & our gardener is very efficient.

37. Aunt Anne—Anne Kinloch (Lee) Marshall (1800–1864), R. E. Lee's sister.

West Point

Robert E. Lee was appointed superintendent of the United States Military Academy and brevetted lieutenant colonel in May 1852, but did not assume his duties until September of that year. His family joined him in late August. The house provided for the head of the Academy was pleasant in every way but Agnes was homesick for her beloved Arlington. Her experience had been limited to visits to family and friends in Virginia and Maryland, and the adjustment to her new "northern" home was at first not easy. She was rising thirteen, at the awkward age of being no longer a child and not yet a young woman. The reader will enjoy watching her develop rather quickly from a shy little girl weeping on the stairs because the cadets "frighten her so" into a young lady who a few months later has "so many intimate acquaintances" in her brother Custis' graduating class.

Students of the Civil War will note with particular interest the names of many cadets who later became prominent on both sides of that conflict and many, alas, who did not survive.

*Robert Edward Lee as superintendent of the United States Military
Academy, painted at West Point by Robert W. Weir, Professor of Drawing at
the Academy.*
Courtesy of Mrs. W. Hunter deButts.

Sept. 13th.

I have not written for some time but I can't. I am perfectly miserable here, I know I ought not to write this but I can't help it. O if my Grandma had not died! O if I only could live at Arlington! O if I could only see that peaceful spot in the woods dearer than anywhere else. But it is so wicked to murmur I can't have everything I wish, so I must hush & look forward to that little star of hope next summer! Fitzhugh has left for school. Grandpa & Papa took a tour to Niagara.[38]

Oct. 18th.

My poor neglected journal, I have forgotten you for more than a month. Many events have transpired perhaps the greatest is my precious Grandpa has left us. Mamma went with him to New York where they remained several days to visit the Chrystal palace & then she returned to her present residence. Grandpa *home*. Annie & I take music & french lessons. Our music master is Mr. Apelles leader of the band, an excellent teacher no doubt but he gives me such long hard exercises & makes me *thrump* so I don't enjoy his lessons much. "French" is ever so nice. We go three times a week to Mr. Agnel.[39] He is not strict but teaches so thoroughly. There are three in the class besides ourselves.

20th.

I don't believe I have yet said anything of "the Point" as it is styled by the natives—& just now turning back I discover I have omitted

38. Tour to Niagara—Lee was worried about Mr. Custis' remaining alone at Arlington after his wife's death and was attempting to interest him in living with the family in New York. Mr. Custis soon returned to Arlington, however.
39. Mr. Agnel—Hyacinth R. Agnel was Professor of French at West Point.

to record the events of our journey after we left Balt. What an omission in the narrative of my unremarkable life but I must be brief. We left B—— Friday night. I had a delightful journey. There was an exquisite moon which seemed so calm herself that this tended to soothe my agitated feelings. I was so excited I could not sleep until long after midnight. We arrived in New York at five next morning & went immediately to the Frances Skitty, a large & handsome boat, to proceed to W.P. I was completely worn out & though the scenery was beautiful fell asleep before we were half way. West Point is a beautiful place, though not to my eyes like Arlington, an impartial judge might *perhaps* think it prettier.

The great virtue here is everything is so neat & clean. Our house is quite large & convenient. We have a fine garden with a pond in it & several meadows. There is quite a nice greenhouse with a splendid lemon tree in it.

6th Nov.

I was interupted last Sunday & now will continue my description of this place. We are about the centre of a row of houses facing the plain. To our right are the cadet barracks, the academic building containing the riding & fencing halls section rooms etc., a little beyond turning again to the right are the mess halls, the hospital & residences. Continuing on a straight line with barracks is the Chapel. We have a fine minister (presbyterian) Mr. Sprole.[40] Next is a very handsome library building. The hotel is opposite across the plain. Camp town & the soldiers' barrack are to our left. The mountains rise beautifully behind us. We walk every day either among them or around "Flirtation" a celebrated walk beyond the

40. Mr. Sprole—William T. Sprole (d. 1883) was the chaplain and a professor at West Point.

plain, just by the river. I fear no description of mine can convey the smallest idea of its beauty. It is a made walk but everything around is so wild & solitary you might imagine art had never been there. In many places the walk is cut through the rock which renders it the more picturesque & magnificent. Sometimes you tread the side of a precipice (such as "lover's leap) again you saunter up an avenue of foliage, then the water lashes almost the very rocks which support your path. Most of the walk is high above the river, but you have exquisite views of it all along. One large rock descends in an inclined plane to the watersedge & I love dearly to run to the very brink of danger. Near is Gee's point—where the cadets go swimming. The rock there descends perpendicularly for two hundred feet & one or two cadets have been drowned. The cemetery is in a commanding spot overlooking the river but higher up beyond the bend. The monuments are handsome but too crowded.

Mrs. Symington & Cousin Laura Stuart are here. John & Eliza were married last Monday & have gone on a wedding tour to Baltimore.

8th Tuesday.

Last Sat. Papa had a large dinner party to some of his classmates, it was at first intended for a gentleman's dinner or "he dinner" as Papa calls them, but Mrs. S's arrival induced Mamma to go in. John the elegant being absent the young ladies played waiter, arranging the table & ornaments. It is such nice work to fix a handsome dinner, but to be present is not to my taste. We also arrange for cadet suppers every Sat. evening, they to be sure need not be very exquisite but must be just right for Papa's scrutinizing eye.

I have met a great many cadets, but it frightens me so, I am so dreadfully diffident I believe Annie & I generally sitting on the steps & having a good cry than remaining in the parlour to enjoy their society. I know Mr. Stuart[41] & Mr. Turnbull Custis'[42] roommate quite well & like them both.

Dec. 1st.

Laura Stuart left us with Aunt Nannie Lee[43] last Tuesday week. Grandpa writes constantly has even written to me & now to Annie. Laura says he keeps the keys himself & gets out all the things. O may God spare his life is my earnest prayer—that we may meet in the dear old halls of home once more.

I should like to write longer but Annie is waiting for me to retire, & perhaps 'tis best I should too, for we rise at gunfire & breakfast at half past six o'clock for Pa must be at his office at seven.

Nov. [Dec.] 4th.

I have a few minutes to write which I will embrace. It is very cold, real winter, it seems to me I am always writing or talking of winter & cold but I am constantly thinking of & dreading it.

We all went to the lower church last Friday. Bishop Wainwright preached & confirmed thirteen persons, among them Emily Henry.

---

41. Mr. Stuart—James E. B. Stuart, '54. Stuart was a favorite of Lee's. He later commanded the Cavalry Corps of the Army of Northern Virginia until his death at Yellow Tavern in 1864.
42. Mr. Turnbull—Charles Nesbit Turnbull, '54. During the war he rose to the rank of brevetted colonel in the U.S. Army Corps of Engineers.
43. Aunt Nannie Lee—Anna Maria (Mason) Lee (1811–1898), R. E. Lee's sister-in-law.

Mary Custis Lee, by Auguste Hervieu. This portrait was done in the 1850s.
Courtesy of Mrs. Frederick Zimmer.

Dec. 29th.

I have not written for a long time so must commence now.

The cadets have had another dialectic meeting, but I did not go this time though Mr. Sheppard[44] & Hancock Taylor[45] were both to speak which was an inducement. Next came the holidays. Christmas eve being Saturday we invited all the first class to a little party. I had a pretty nice time but a dreadful headache. To be surrounded by several cadets at once is no very pleasant feeling, but I am overcoming my bashfulness a little. I don't know it is any great advantage in one so young. I fear I am getting corrupted by the world. If I could only have staid at A—— a few years longer, but it must be for the best though I can't see through it. Several young ladies came to our assistance in entertaining, Rebecca Sprole, Miss Roberts, Miss Agnel & the Misses Cozzens, and two pretty matrons Mrs. G. W. Smith[46] & Mrs. Baird.[47]

Sat. night I was up very late & proportionably sleepy in the morning, but Mildred sprang into our bed at four so there was no more sleep for that Christmas morning. I received a pretty ring from Papa with my initial on it & several other pretty gifts. Custis had an additional day to be with us which was very pleasant. Tuesday we all went to the riding hall & saw him ride for the first time. Yesterday was Holy Innocence day & a festival for the school children of that church. The children came at five, then such noise & crowding & fun. The tree looked beautifully & the tables were loaded. They seemed to enjoy themselves as much as possi-

---

44. Mr. Sheppard—Samuel T. Shepperd, '54, died at Fort Leavenworth in 1855.
45. Hancock Taylor—probably Joseph H. Taylor, '56, served in the Federal army, becoming a brevetted colonel, and dying in Omaha in 1885.
46. Mrs. G. W. Smith—Gustavus W. Smith was Principal Assistant Professor of Engineering. He later became a major general in the Confederate Army.
47. Mrs. Baird—Mrs. Absalom Baird.

ble. We played waiters & I am sure I stuffed them & their pockets. A snow storm came up as we were leaving so we rode up in the omnibus. I had a nice time but was very tired.

Jan. 22nd 1854

I am very sorry I did not write on the first of this month as I fully intended to do but—I have no good excuse & I won't give a bad one. What a different creature I am this year. In one year I have learnt & experienced a great deal. I feel differently too; young as I am I must sit up & talk & walk as a young lady and be constantly greeted with ladies do this & that & think so all as if I was twenty but enough of this.

New Years morning Mr. Sprole gave a very good sermon "And the Lord said set thy House in order for thou shalt die." He is a fine preacher but a little hard on the cadets & too pointed in his remarks. Annie was sick all last week & I head nurse though she has not done half justice to my efficiency I am sure she is better.

Feb. 2nd.

Papa gave a dinner last Tuesday to Gen. Robles of the Mexican Army. To make sure of being out of the way Annie & I with Neva Bartlett bent our steps towards Flirtation. It was beautiful in the snow. We met Mrs. G. W. & Mr. Pegram,[48] a great friend of hers. Also Fitzhugh Lee,[49] our first cousin. He got into a scrape poor

---

48. Mr. Pegram—John Pegram, '54. He became a brigadier general in the Confederate Army and was killed in February 1865.
49. Fitzhugh Lee—the son of Smith Lee. At this time he was in trouble for leaving the Academy without permission. He became a major general in the Confederate Cavalry, and was elected governor of Virginia in 1885.

fellow & his punishment is walking post of course & he is not allowed to visit so I scarcely ever see him & he is more a stranger than almost any cadet in the corps.

The winter gaieties have commenced, officers' concerts, cadets' ditto & dialectics—parties & hops which are frequent of course I don't attend.

Feb. 9th.

I am all alone for two hours tonight, so will write to wile away the time. I believe I commenced upon the W.P. gaieties but was in-terupted by my music teacher. The officers concerts are held in the Library & are very fine. The cadets have one every Sat. eve-ning in the fencing hall. The room is much too small so the music is very loud, but it is necessary to have it almost deafening to drown the noise made in the background by some cadets who appear to come for that purpose. Even those who accompany ladies keep up a stream of conversation, hollowing in ones ears till they are half cracked, still I enjoy them, & I fear the leader, our Music Master, thinks his two poor pupils who are usually con-signed to the front seats, are rather merry to be attentive listeners.

We always have a no. of cadets at our house every Sat. evening. Last Saturday Papa invited some nine or ten from the 3rd class. None were talkative or self possessed except Mr. Sprigg Carroll,[50] who made up for the others. His gloves are the subject of great admiration. I sat by a Mr. Houston[51] a long time a pale intellectual

---

50. Mr. Sprigg Carroll—probably Samuel S. Carroll, '56. He served as a colonel in the Ohio Volunteers and rose to be major general. He died in 1893.
51. Mr. Houston—David C. Houston, '56. He became a brevetted colonel in the U.S. Army during the war.

youth head of his class but at that time even his name was unknown to me, so it was charming!

We know almost all of Custis' class, the 1st, & many in the other three. Brother has been always head I believe so we are quite proud of him as he is several years younger than those next to him & then he was born & educated in Virginia where 'tis thought people are so lazy.

The cadet uniform is all grey in winter—white pants in summer, but the sombre hue is much relieved by the gilt bullet buttons & cheverins on the officers.

I do hope we wont stay here longer than this summer. I wish Annie & I could have a governess & study at Arlington, but I suppose it cannot be. How I *do* want to see my home. I pray every morning & night we may all meet there in the summer it is almost my dearest wish. O to be once more in Grandpa's arms, once more in the dear old house and more than all to be once again at my Grandma's grave to kiss the sod & think of her who is in Heaven. Then the dear old servants, & my pets my bunnys, one poor little thing is dead, my chickens, my cats, pigeons, garden in fact everything in & near home I anticipate with the greatest delights, & all my southern friends too. It snowed hard last Wed. morning so we had every prospect for some fine sleighrides but our hopes have been blighted by a warm rain. Even now the river is frozen hard so that sleighs pass over it.

March 9th.

Fitzhugh has not received his appointment after all his trouble. I am so sorry it is *such* a disappointment to him. He is so anxious to enter the Army in some way. I remember last summer when he used to stand watching dress parade he would involuntarily exclaim "O if I was only one of them." The weather is delightful, even dress parades & guard mounting have commenced & we have violets in bloom. Cousin Markie[52] sent me some crocus' the other day, she has been staying with Grandpa all winter.

March 15th.

The weather is delightful now more like May. Annie & I have resumed our mountain walks, & took a long steep climb up Redoubt Mountain the other day. Last Tuesday Mamma, Annie, Milly & I went to see Custis' class ride. C—— has a very pretty little black horse named "Sultan" that almost flies. Mr. Sackett[53] says 'he goes too fast he is afraid he will fall.' Mr. Pegram was riding a horse that was as stubborn as a mule. He will not move against his will. The more he is whipped the more contrary he becomes, backs upon the whip, turns around & around & will not do as they wish him to. He was finally given to Mr. S. Drake—one of the very best riders in the corps, but the horse was so hot, mad & frightened that he threw him without however hurting him. The soldiers then caught him by the nose & pulled him around which seemed to subdue him a little. I was very much interested, it is perfectly fascinating to watch the riding. But I must stop now & look at drill!

18th.

It has become very cold again. We all went to church this morning except Mary who has had something the matter with her foot ever since Christmas & Milly who has not yet recovered from the

52. Cousin Markie—Martha Custis Williams (1827–1899), who was staying at Arlington with Mr. Custis.
53. Mr. Sackett—Delos Bennett Sackett (1822?–1885) was Assistant Instructor of Cavalry Tactics.

whooping cough. We had a very good sermon. I always like the end of Mr. Sprole's sermons better than the beginnings. There was one poor cadet whom all the parson's eloquence could not rouze. He sat near our pew & I think some of my attention was drawn off watching him. He would give a tremendous yawn, shake himself & try every means to arouze, but it was of no use he would sink back upon the bench & go fast asleep.—But Custis has come so I must stop.

28th May.

I left off very abruptly last time I wrote which was ever so long ago. We have had no Spring yet & this is the last of it, but the weather is beautiful now. June is a great month here. The cadets are examined. Many pass & go into the next higher class, while some are *found* (that is deficient) & are sent away. The first class graduate, & the new appointments compose the fourth. They go by the name of "plebes." Poor fellows, they are teazed, tormented & tricked almost out of their lives. They are not expected to enter into any of the enjoyments of the other classes, their comrades look down upon them with much scorn & pity! All, the other cadets say for their good they have had their turn & feel all the better for it. Perhaps a little would do no harm but I know it is carried too far & tell them it is only out of revenge for what they have suffered. Custis' class graduates this year, I am very sorry, for he was so near us here we could see him often. Probably when his furlough of two or three months is over, he may be ordered to California or New Mexico & then there is no telling when we will see him again. Besides we have so many intimate acquaintances in his class. I suspect a great deal of our interest in cadets will be lost when Custis is not here. Mamma, Sister & Milly went home about the 1st of this month. Sister's foot was better, she had a buckskin shoe made & bore the journey pretty well. Grandpa was quite well. He has presented the President or Congress with some revolutionary colors[54] & had dined with the Pres., which was some excitement for him. All the servants were save dear old Mammy, she is failing, I think she must be seventy five. I do hope I will see her once more. Annie & I wanted to go on very much, but it was determined we should finish our lessons here & go on with Custis. We may however wait for Pa for C——, & his class, will want to stop & see the sights & not be encumbered with two girls. We will be two "too many" sure enough.

June 11th.

The examinations have commenced but before I speak of them, I must mention an accident that happened to a first classman Smead,[55] a few weeks before 1st June. It was after a heavy rain when one end of the plain was quite muddy. The two batoons were practicing for the exhibition before the board. Mr. Sackett (the instructor) gave the command to charge but to halt before they reached the mud. The cadets however got excited & commenced racing so furiously they could not halt when they reached the forbidden ground. Smead's horse slipped threw his rider & rolled over him—but fortunately stood perfectly still while Mr. S——'s foot was extricated from the stirrup. He was taken up insensible & his life dispaired of for several days. He lay in a stupor for a week never speaking unless addressed & Dr. Cuyler feared brain fever as all the injury was there & some bruises on his face. But the saying is here, "you can't kill a cadet". It is

54. Revolutionary colors—Custis presented some British and Hessian flags, which had been captured at Trenton and Yorktown and presented to Washington by Congress.
55. Smead—Abner Smead, '54. Smead's recovery was not as complete as Agnes thought; he was still suffering from the fall ten years later. He was with Lee and Stuart at Harpers Ferry in 1859. He became a colonel in the Confederate Army.

certainly true in this case for he has attended all of his examinations & was even at church this morning to hear Mr. Sprole's parting address to the graduating class. His eyes until lately have been very dull & his face deathly pale but he looks better today. I have written a longer account of him than I intended but he interested me so much, though I didn't know him personally, that I couldn't think of anything else for one or two days. I felt *so* sorry for him.

June 18th.

This is Annie's birthday but I suppose she has forgotten all about it.

I must now write something of the examinations which have just passed. The review on the 1st was very fine. One of the most beautiful days I ever saw & felt. After it the board[56] all of the officers and the cadet officers came to our house to partake of a collation. We retreated from the blinds up stairs, as we could not summon up enough courage to appear. The 1st class came up on engineering on the 2nd. We were to meet Capt. & Mrs. Barry (who have been staying with us) at the door but arrived too late! a just disappointment for our tardiness. But we went the next Tuesday with Mrs. G. W. Smith to the examination on Ethics. Every one told me I wouldn't understand one word of National law, but to my great satisfaction I did many words & liked it very much. Custis came out first as he did in Engineering in fact in everything except 3rd in fencing & fourth in riding. 1st in general standing, take him all in all he is a brother any one might be proud of.

We went to several examinations—one in french knowing I was a great scholar! I felt myself a judge. I was rather disappointed in

---

56. Board of Visitors—This board supervised the final exams at the Academy each spring and made a report to Congress. Lee had been on the board before becoming superintendent.

View from the Parade Ground at West Point, from a painting by
George Catlin. The superintendent's house, in which Agnes lived,
is second from the left.
Courtesy of the United States Military Academy Library.

the 1st sect. of the 3rd class which graduated in that branch. Perhaps I expected too much but they did make several inexcusable mistakes such as plural for votre "Votres" & "nous êtes." We attended all the drills riding, fencing etc. Smith Lee has been staying with us. He came up to see Fitz. before going to sea. I have not seen F——. to speak to him for almost six months until a few evenings ago. He is so full of mischief, he is always getting into trouble. Thursday eve. Mr. Clemens (secretary of the boards of visitors) addressed the Dialectic society in the Chapel. Every year a board of gentlemen assemble here to examine into everything so that they may spread over the U.S. "liberal views" of the Academy. Next evening Mr. Bayard made an address to the graduating class—at least it was meant but it was the longest most uninteresting thing about "unlimited extension" etc. stupid to a degree. Then the diplomas were distributed. Custis was not able to receive his in person as he had a violent chill at the time. Poor fellow he has been too sick to go to the last hop, the fireworks, or the last parade. The music at parade was beautiful "Home sweet Home" went to many a heart "Auld lang Syne" chimed in with their feelings—it was so mournful but so sweet. The fireworks were very pretty, were ended by two large tar barrels being set on fire and rolled into Execution hollow! The graduates left Sat. morning. Most of those we knew came in after guard-mounting to say goodbye. They were all in the highest spirits amused themselves & us with the variety in their citizens dress. How we miss them. What will we do next winter without this graduating class. We had so many nice visitors every Sat. evening. Last Saturday was so stupid with only a few second classmen. Custis is staying with us until he gets well.

20th June.

I am writing before breakfast though it is seven. We are not usually so lazy as we finish usually at half past six. But we have Cousin Esther Lewis, Eddy, Conny, & Dainger[57] staying here so we wait their will & pleasure. We were with them three years ago at Audley.[58] I think it was one of the happiest summers I ever passed. There were only herself, My Grandmamma, & Aunt Lewis, & the six boys. But generally I prefer the society of boys—perhaps be-

57. Cousin Esther Lewis, Eddy, Conny, & Dainger—Esther Maria (Coxe) Lewis (d. 1885), Edward Parke Custis Lewis (1837–1892), Charles Conrad Lewis (1839–1859), and Henry Llewellyn Daingerfield Lewis (1843–1893).
58. Audley—Clarke County, Virginia.

cause I am *used* to them, I don't know so much about playing with girls—then you need only be with boys when you feel in the humour for it. Aunt L—— was one of the kindest & best ladies I ever knew. She died several years ago. But I was only ten then; now years of experience & age seems to have passed over my feelings.

Arlington July 16th.

You see I am again at dear old Arlington have been here several weeks. I really am so idle I must be more industrious but it is so hard when one is reading or playing to stop to practice or sew. Papa has come bringing kind messages from our friends at West Point. I really have a kind of home feeling for the place & can look back to the winter we passed there as a very happy period of my long life for I have reached the respectable age of thirteen. How well I remember the first few months. I am naturally so reserved and retiring I used to suffer "agonies." It was no laughing matter then Annie was just as bad many a cry we have had & thought "Woe was the day we left Arlington." We had to see so many strangers particularly gentlemen & cadets have such a way of treating children as grown persons. Of course I was wholly unfit for such a position never aspiring so high, however now I am up to it! I can look back with the air of a stoic upon those *stormy* times & feel myself above such pertubations. Anyone might think from my manner of talking now I had become a perfectly self possessed young lady only let them see me!

But I must put down my pen if it can't write more sense & go to teach my little scholars. We have a considerable number of "ebony mites" as Papa calls them & as no one knows as much as another it makes their instruction very tedious. Well! I have gone down, I insist upon teaching them in classes & yet only one of any class ever arrived at a time so I have employed this odd moment in writing. Aunt Peter died on the 13th July 1854 about two A.M. She was buried at Oaklands the home of one of her sons. She had heart disease but it was principally old age. She was more than seventy five. She led a very active wearing life working hard from preference giving herself no indulgences, but it was long before her strong constitution gave way. She lay dying for three days O what agony for her children. Mamma spent several days at Tudor Place[59] with her. She was Grandpa's last surviving whole sister. O that the last of them may be spared to us a little longer! Aunt Robinson died before I was born. I think Aunt Lewis was Grandpa's favorite sister, she was so kind & winning, no one could help loving her. She was so beautiful, retaining it even when I knew her. But I never shall forget Aunt Peter's kindness to us last Spring in our trying affliction. She saw to everything did everything & was so considerate. She was rather cold & harsh usually & I had always stood rather in awe of her, but I felt very *very* grateful for her kindness then and loved her very much afterwards. We have good reason to believe she went to Heaven for everyone has faults & we could not expect her to be more perfect than the rest of mankind.

18th.

I am going to try to write twice a week in my journal for the improvement of my style & handwriting, though I got into such a habit of scribling at W.P. I fear it will be impossible to break myself of it. But if my handwriting was injured my music, french, manners & habits were certainly improved. Mr. Apelles talk me what it was to *practice* & *understand* a piece. Mr. Agnel's praises are sung on every side. Studying french was only agreable play, but it made me feel dreadfully to have an imperfect lesson. I don't think it

59. Tudor Place—The Peter house in Georgetown, at this time owned by Britannia Wellington (Peter) Kennon (1815–1911).

happened very often. He taught so pleasantly was so lenient & gentlemanly we were always ready to "go to french." I think we learnt a great deal. I conquered a good deal of my diffidence & learned to conduct myself in society with tolerable self-possession. Then we rose before gun fire & finished breakfast before seven for Papa had to be at the office then. Cold bread for breakfast & all of our meals wholesome & simple. I missed the servants at home so much to mend my clothes but necessity is a good master & ingenuity soon assisted us. We took long walks through wind & snow & would come back with our cheeks glowing & feeling as well & happy as possible, unless, as happened sometimes, our ears & noses were half frozen with the cold. But I never felt so well before that winter.

Aunt Agy died a week or two ago from apoplexy she left many children. One married to William in Liberia & Eliza is now at Newport with John & her Emmeline! Pa, Ma, & Mildred have gone to spend the day with Aunt Nannie Lee & go on for the night to Cousin Lucy Mason's. Sister's foot is better. Dr. Coolidge[60] is attending her, says she must be very quiet & not put her foot to the ground. Annie & I sometimes make a chair with our hands & carry her but she is pretty heavy. Mr. Turnbull came yesterday & spent the night.

21st.

With great reluctance I commence my journal for it is *really so hot* I can scarcely breathe. I feel like doing nothing but exclaim O tis *so* hot! but that is not very cooling. We expect Aunt Maria to dinner but I do not think she will brave this weather. I want to see her & all of our *old* friends very much but one of our carriage horses is only just recovering from a lameness of long duration, so we have been nowhere. I really can't write, I am half distracted with heat.

60. Dr. Coolidge—Dr. Richard Henry Coolidge (d. 1866).

Tuesday.

I have found I have neither matter nor inclination to write twice a week, nor have my studies been kept up very regularly. I am now in a "don't care" state or rather resigned to my fate. We have expostulated and begged and reasoned—Papa is inexorable. We leave for W.P. on Saturday with him—that is Sister, Annie, Roone, Rob & myself. The rest follow with Grandpa in a few weeks. Sister is only a little better, we are anxious for her to see Dr. Barnes[61] again. We spend a few days with Aunt Anne in Balt. in her new house. That is the only bright spot.

Papa, Mamma & Mary have gone up to Ravensworth to spend a day or two & bring nos chers frères home, who have been gadding about for two or three weeks quite forgetting their sisters I suppose!

Sunday eve. Dec. 31st.

The last day of 1854! What reflections it brings with it. How much of it have I employed well—how much wasted? I am afraid if I answer truly far *far* the greater portion has been mispent or wasted. But I must stop moralizing for a while & give some idea where I am this last day of the year. Of course not at my own old Arlington but at W.P. sitting down at the same old writing desk in the dining room. Let me glance briefly at the past. The party I mentioned in my last left home the veritable day after all of our loved haunts have been visited each servant, with the parting gift, have been told good-bye with the wish 'I hope I'll see you *next* summer well & happy' how truly those words came from my heart—even the animals seemed to look afection through their dumb eyes. Those we left behind were hugged & kissed & told

61. Dr. Barnes—Joseph K. Barnes, assistant surgeon at West Point.

"good-bye" but we expected to seem them *soon again.* In a short time we were steaming on to Balt. where we spent a few days with Aunt Anne.[62] She is so sweet & kind she makes every one love her. She was so well too, for her walking all about the house. They had just moved to their new house which is a nice new one on McCulloch St. It was so pleasant also to see all our old friends, who seemed very glad to meet us again & were very kind & sociable. We travelled on at night to New York. The heat in the day was insupportable. Papa & Rooney carried Sister, Annie her crutches, Rob, little Tip, who sat up grandly in his arms, I the cloaks of the party numbering three or four large & heavy. Tip was a troublesome baby & in the interval of the departure of the boat was hurriedly restored to his Mistress Miss Helen, with the hope that his health had been much benefited by his summer sojourn in Virginia.

Our party excited much sympathy as we came on. Whenever we had to change cars the Conductor would scream to "Jack" or "Bill" etc. to come & help a lady who couldn't walk instantly two or three great men would rush up & lift us, cloaks, crutches, dogs, & people up or down whether we would or no.

West Point was perfectly dried up it had hardly rained for two months & did not for as many more. I was only a little glad to get back. Our cook was the only domestic left, & Mr. Van Ranseleer & his two daughters arriving Annie & I had to become "Jacks of all trades." They had returned from the Springs to attend the last cadet hop which is considered something great here, but could get in at neither overflowing hotel, so Pa offered them a resting place here. Both of the young ladies especially the younger Cornelia were very pretty & nice. Papa took us one evening over to the Iron foundry just by Cold Spring. The visit was very interesting & the rowing across delightful. It was the first I had been although so near. But I am too tired to write more.

62. Aunt Anne—Mrs. Marshall was an invalid most of her life.

Closer view of the superintendent's house, taken in 1870
after a porch had been added.
Courtesy of the United States Military Academy Library.

March 11th.

We have just returned from the "Holy Innocents" a little episcopal chapel—very pretty but a little too much like a catholic one, about a mile & a half from West Point proper—but I must again go back & commence where I left off. Grandpa came on with Mamma spent a month with us then Custis escorted him home. He returned soon to tell us good-bye before starting for Savannah as he thought. But they detained him in Wash. until about a week ago to copy some drawings of Ft. Clinch.[63] He stayed at home until New

63. Fort Clinch—Custis had been stationed at this fort on Amelia Island, Georgia.

Year & then took a room in the city. Helen Peters came up about a month before Christmas & was induced to remain until the morning of that day. Christmas eve, or rather Sat. evening which was celebrated as such we had a grand party to all of our cadet acquaintances. I enjoyed myself very much & the entertainment broke up at the seasonable hour of ten!

Papa gave us very pretty work boxes for "Christmas gift", Rob & Milly were loaded as usual. Next Tuesday eve. the juveniles of the Point were feted at our house. But New Years day was the great day. From morning till night the house was filled by officers & cadets, dinner was dispensed with by most of us while "sweets" of all kinds supplied its place.

I had ever so much fun—such a nice time. Literally "gabbled" or listened to it all day. Tired as we were we spent the evening with Helen Bratt, where we talked a *great deal* more & went to bed perfectly "overkim as it were." Next Tuesday Jimmy Cuyler,[64] the Surgeon's son, gave a grand party to the juveniles. One of the bandsmen played for dancing, the supper was very fine— turkey, oysters, sangaree, marmelade ice cream, cake, mottoes & all things nice. We danced, played games & had a fine time. It broke up at twelve so see how fashionable we youngsters are. But we four young people prudently left about eleven. Maggie & Helen returned to school next morning.

We have gone to many of the concerts this winter both officers & cadets. Some are very fine. There is one favorite piece the "Nebbilbilder" or some such thing. It is divided into four parts—"The Sunrise, Storm, The gypsy camp & Coronation celebration." The cow-bells, the lowing of the kine, the rain every sound is brought in to perfection. The storm is *grand.* There is a beautiful claronet performer in the band. We have had two "dialectics" one on the

64. Jimmy Cuyler—Dr. John Meck Cuyler (d. 1884) was the chief medical officer.

22nd. The national airs were very welcome I haven't heard them for a long time. Rooney went on to Wash. during his vacation to get his appointment as a cadet, but couldn't do it. He has borne up bravely, consoling himself with some sage remarks of Custis'. We have heard from him since his return to Cambridge, he promises to do great things.

I must now say something about St. Valentine's day. Missives flew back & forth the whole week. Rob & Mil. each received & sent at least a dozen. Most of them original without much regard to rhyme or metre. Sister had a good many too. Annie & I considered ourselves much neglected I only had one. But the quality of this one! I was compared to sugar—clarafied at that, molasses, honey, & all things sweet. It was easy to discover the Author, as he had first written his name & then erased it so badly I could make it out. But the youth was always so much overcome afterwards & apparently so shocked that I was not, I never mentioned it to him. The Saturday after the day Mamma gave a Valentine party to the cadets. Verses, suited to their characters as nearly as possible were written with the cadet's name inside, they were then folded up & handed round in a basket for each lady to draw one & as there were so many masculines some ladies had two or even three Valentines. Mine was Cadet-Lieut. Junius B. Wheeler![65] about the greatest lady's man in the room. I showed my appreciation of the favor the kind Saint had shown me by behaving just as badly as such a retiring young damsel could behave. All that week we had dinners, parties, & small dinners, indeed—we have had so many, averaging more than one a week, that the whole family are heartily sick of them. We declare they are Pa's *delight* but he maintains he dislikes them very much.

I must mention one more fact then stop. It is, we are no longer

65. Junius B. Wheeler—Junius Brutus Wheeler (1831?–1886).

in the Engineers[66] but the cavalry.[67] Pa was Capt. in the former with the bvt. rank of col. He is now Lieut. Col. of Cav. retaining of course his bvt. rank. My first information was returning from Mr. Agnel's with our french books, I saw Mr. Stockton who called out "Miss Lee, Miss Lee, do you know your father is *Col. Lieut-Colonel* in one of these new regiments." & he showed me his name in the paper he was reading.

I sprang on to tell the news first at home but Dr. Cuyler was just informing Mamma so I ran upstairs to be first there. At first I was delighted, the idea of promotion, of leaving W.P. changing our corps etc. was something new & charming. But second thoughts— Papa's going way out West, and—and leaving West Point, that I now almost consider as home was very sad. We all regret it now. Papa is glad to leave here & of course likes promotion but doesn't like giving up the Eng. corps, in which he has been for more than twenty years, & then to break up & leave us for those western wilds. We have received a no. of letters today, from Grandpa, Cousin Markie Custis (who is in Atlanta looking for a lost trunk) Capt. Cullom[68] (congratulating Pa on his new dignities, but deploring his leaving their corps) & Helen Peters.

"French" is flourishing. Our class is composed of Willie & Neva Bartlett, Jimmy Cuyler, Annie & I & Vinnie Agnel. Music is progressing too. Mr. Apelles has condescended at last to give us each a polka, a real bona fide polka. They are "tolrob". I have had several nice sleigh rides but hope there will be no more snow.

66. Engineering Corps—In addition to sentimental preference after a career spent with the Engineers, Lee probably preferred them because they were considered the elite branch of the army.
67. Cavalry—Lee had been made second-in-command of the 2nd Cavalry, formed to protect Texas settlers from Indian attacks.
68. Capt. Cullom—George W. Cullum was Instructor of Practical Military Engineering and Commandant of Sappers, Miners, and Pontoniers. He later became superintendent of the Academy.

13th.

Last Saturday eve we made our first acquaintance with plebes. About a dozen were invited. They were very nice boys it hardly becomes *me* to call them boys, but, though young in years, my residence at W.P. has given me the experience of an ancient & enables me to look down upon young people generally from a great height! They were introduced as usual "en masse" & as all were strangers this time it was a perfect puzzle to find out their names even with the best attention. One I talked to before tea, at tea, & after tea but in vain until a kind friend breathed his name. To another's Pa assisted me, still another finally opened a book, his eye resting on the word Phillip (for want of a topic I suppose) observed "there by adding an *s* you make my name." I paid a just tribute to his happily chosen subject by confessing I was hopelessly wondering to whom I was talking. And this we have to go through nearly every Saturday evening, the devices varying with the subjects.

March 18th.

We had a fine sermon from Mr. Sprole this morning. The text "But one sinner destroyeth much good." Eccle. IX.18. I was uncontrolably sleepy at first but it soon rouzed me. As usual it was very severe though a little softened towards the end. He told them (for he always preaches to the cadets only) if they were determined to be wicked, if they *must* swear to go to some cave or desert island, where no one could be harmed by their example. In the midst of his discourse looking very sternly & severely down into the church he said "that he asked that young man to close his book & listen to him—he asked him kindly feeling sure he would do it." I hope it did good but I am afraid it only made him angry. The cadets as a body behave very well, but some few—I hope very

Artillery Drill at West Point, 1860.
Courtesy of the United States Military Academy Library.

few—bring books & read during the sermon, which is certainly very wrong. We have just heard from Rooney & Custis. The latter is staying at Mrs. Lowe's waiting for Capt. Gilmer.[69] I hope he will answer my letter soon. I do love to receive letters.

Maggie & Helen came up last Friday & will we hope again in two weeks for the Easter holiday. Yesterday morn. on jumping out of bed we found the ground covered with snow, & still falling fast. We were much disappointed as we had anticipated walking around with them a good deal. We prepared ourselves however to

69. Capt. Gilmer—Jeremy F. Gilmer was in charge of the construction at Amelia Island.

go out, & though the snow changed into rain, like true West Pointers not minding wind or weather we sallied forth, & with some persuading, particularly by Helen, induced them to spend the evening with us to meet some first-classmen. As usual the anticipation was dreadful. It seems strange to me it should always be so, though for nearly two years I have seen cadets every Sat. evening & afternoon. When I get excited & am talking to those I like & who amuse me I forget, in my enjoyment my miserable feelings. This evening was dreaded as much as ever, but turned out pleasently enough. Mr. Dick.[70] made himself particularly agreeable. Messrs. Wheeler & Hill[71] were sick. Many of the other invited ones had got into trouble. Fitz. & his friend "Wrag" among them. The girls looked very well, Helen almost *lovely*. But I go & tell them good-bye, they leave for school to-morrow.

April 1st.

The wind roze this morning, while we were at the lower church, & was so violent we had often to turn our backs walking home until the gust past over. Cadets Webb[72] & Childs[73] walked home with us to Mr. d'Oremieux's[74] when they had to run to be in time for the drum. Mamma stopped at Dr. Cuyler's who has been long sick, so Annie & I faced the fierce north wind alone which comes down

70. Mr. Dick—George McGaw Dick, '55. Dick died while serving under Lee in Texas.

71. Hill—James Hoffman Hill (1834?–1890) or Robert C. Hill, both '55, and both of whom served in the Army of the Confederacy.

72. Webb—Alexander S. Webb, '55. He later became a brevetted major general in the U.S. Army.

73. Childs—Frederick L. Childs, '55. Childs later joined the Confederate Army, served as a lieutenant colonel, and lived until 1895.

74. Mr. d'Oremieux—Theophile D'Oremieux was principal Assistant Professor of French.

between the mountains in all its fury. Sister went with Papa & Mil. to the chapel, for the first time. Her foot is much better though getting well slowly.

Arlington April 16th 1855.

O only to think I am once more at my dear old home! My precious Arlington! But as I write a feeling of sorrow mingles with my joy for we have left West Point—dear West Point (what an unromantic name!) with no definite idea of ever seeing it again. The beautiful mountains, the deep rocky Hudson with its pure dark waters, the fresh mountain air, the buildings, the band, the parades, the people—down to the very flagstaff & sidewalk with their innumerable associations have all past from our sight perhaps for ever.—But I must begin where I left off which was a week before leaving the Point "pausing", as our Parson used to say, at New York & Baltimore until we reached here.

So one Monday morning bright and early we commenced to pack & sell everything we could lay our hands on. We retained the furniture of the parlours & library, & many other things. As to packing don't speak of it going up & down from garret to cellar was soon regarded as *nothing*. The plan decided on was to leave Monday the 9th spend a few days en route & reach home by Saturday. Military men—consequently their families can pay little regard to times so though Passion week we still had to pack pack. We were soon reduced to some down stairs furniture & a few beds. There were two deaths during the week, the first Cadet Kernes[75] of the fourth or fifth class. He died very suddenly. A little unwell he went to the Mess hall one evening & expired a few hours afterwards. Mr. Sprole asked him if there was anything he could do for him. He said "Yes let me put my arms round your

75. Kernes—Probably Theodore Koerner (1837?–1855).

neck" he did so & breathed his last. Poor young fellow he felt so far away from those he knew & loved or perhaps the river of death looked dark. He said "he knew it was best it was God's will & his Mother had brought him up a christian." So I hope he is with His Heavenly Father now.

The Military funeral was very imposing. His body was first taken to the Chapel, then wrapped in the flag of our country was borne to the Cemetary. The band came first playing such a beautiful dead March, next the escort composed of his own class with crape on the left arm, then the hearse with a few grouped round it, next last the rest of the corps in undress & last the Army officers in full uniform. They marched slowly round the plain on to the Cemetary, when we heard the salute of three guns reverberate through the beautiful mountains beyond.

We managed to have everything sufficiently packed up by Saturday evening to part with our cadet friends.

I was in a perfect "gale" as Grandpa would say & laughed & talked the whole time. I scarcely ever had so much fun. I told them I was dying with grief at the idea of parting, had been dissolved in tears the whole morning, & had just now controled myself enough to say good-bye, but expected to be in the same condition when they left, my red & swollen eyes would testify to what I had asserted. They all remarked my apparent self control was most admirably feigned & my eyes most deceptive. They begged & we promised we would return in the summer to attend the hops & I believe some think we really will. Numerous promises were given & exchanged at last after many good-byes last words & affectionate shakes of the hand they left. My parting with Mr. W. was peculiarly affecting. On entering he rushed up to me seized my hand exclaiming "Miss Agnes do I see thee in health?" & when leaving pressed it long and tenderly, then breathed out with as much present anguish but still a faint tone of joy for the future as he could summon for the occasion Good-bye O *good-bye* till I meet thee this summer in Virginia!" But one must know him to appreciate that parting scene. I think what must have put me in such high spirits was just as our visitors were coming I had a perfect romp in the parlours with Chudie.[76] Very undignified I admit for a young lady just fourteen to have a romp with a grey coat & brass buttons a 2nd classmen too, but it is a painful fact & his first cousinship is my sole excuse. Chudie & Sister sallied out to visit the Misses Tompson just as they *knew* cadets would be coming in, so we turned back by Cadets Church[77] & Hill. I sat a few minutes making myself as stupid as possible when to my great relief Sister asked me to get her Lt. Cogswell's[78] photograph & some others she had upstairs. I jumped up but on returning couldn't summon courage to enter the library alone so went into the front parlour & found my cousin with Annie both having absconded shortly after our visitors arrival. I put my hands behind me and excited his curiosity so much he promised if I would only show him what I had he would go in the room with me. But once having got the pictures he neither would go nor give them back to me. Then such chasing & laughing until I got half provoked. The bell rang again. I was perplexed I couldn't go in the room by myself when it was so full & C—— vowed he felt much worse than I did. After an hours delay I procured all the photographs & he promised to open the door for me if I would go in first which was done with much solemnity. But we had really laughed so much I feared I wouldn't be able to raise another smile, however a few hints at Fitz's behaviour & his pleading winks for silence soon loosened my risibles. I looked out on parade that evening for the *last* time. How strangely it sounded as I repeated to myself 'my last parade' I couldn't realize it. Annie & I had invitations to Mrs.

76. Chudie—a nickname for Fitzhugh Lee.
77. Church—John R. Church, '55. He later joined the Confederate Army, and was killed in 1863.
78. Cogswell—Milton Cogswell (1825?–1882).

Church's, Mrs. Barnes' & Mrs. Walker's,[79] we accepted the first. Sister & Chudie went to Mrs. B——'s, Ma to Mrs. Walker's, Pa over the river to Mr. Kemble's Rob. to Mrs. Dick Smith's[80] & Mildred passed the evening with her friend Minnie Sprole. Were we not for that eve. truly a divided family. Maggie & Helen had brought up with them two friends—Sallie Parks & Camilla Waters to spend the Easter holidays. So we six girls & a few cadets made a pleasant though quiet party. Though kindly pressed to spend the night as we still had a *bed* we declined. Mildred & Rob. did stay with their respective friends. Friday night I had a farewell talk of about three hours with Bunny[81] wasn't that "charment"?

I see I have been entirely too minute recording in black & white a great deal of nonsense but everything connected with those last days at the Point now seems of double importance for they were the *last*!

17th.

I must try to be more brief to-day. Sunday morning we looked on our last inspection then Annie & I went to the Chapel where Sister, who had spent the night at Mrs. Barnes joined us. Being Easter & Communion Sunday Pa and Ma attended the H.I. Dr. Potts preached from the text beginning "The kingdom of Heaven cometh not with observation etc." Luke XII.20.21 His manner is so much milder & softer than our parsons it was most interesting. I looked on the chapel for the *last* time & Mr. Wier's[82] beautiful

---

79. Mrs. Walker—Bvt. Lt. Col. William H. T. Walker was Commandant of Cadets and Instructor of Infantry Tactics.
80. Mrs. Dick Smith—Richard W. Smith taught drawing at West Point.
81. Bunny—Orton Williams, although there is no record that he had enrolled in the Military Academy.
82. Mr. Wier—Robert W. Weir taught drawing at West Point. He painted one of two portraits made of Lee before the war.

OFFICIAL REGISTER

OF THE

OFFICERS AND CADETS

OF THE

U. S. MILITARY ACADEMY,

WEST POINT, NEW YORK.

JUNE, 1854.

7

FIRST CLASS—46 MEMBERS—1854.

Order of general merit	Names	State	Date of admission	Age (Years)	Age (Mon)	Demerit for six months
*1	G. W. Custis Lee	At Large	July 1, '50	17	6	18
*2	Henry L. Abbot	Mass.	do	18	10	7
*3	Thomas H. Ruger	Wis.	do	17	2	12
*4	Oliver O. Howard	Me.	Sept. 1, '50	19	9	7
*5	Thomas J. Treadwell	N. H.	July 1, '50	18	2	62
6	Charles N. Turnbull	At Large	Sept. 1, '50	17	1	10
7	James Deshler	Ala.	July 1, '50	17	4	30
8	Henry W. Closson	Vt.	Sept. 1, '50	18	2	25
9	Judson D. Bingham	Ia.	July 1, '50	19	1	22
10	John Pegram	Va.	do	18	5	91
11	Charles G. Rogers	Va.	do	18	8	49
12	Thomas J. Wright	At Large	do	17	5	75
13	James E. B. Stuart	Va.	do	17	4	66
14	Archibald Gracie, Jr.	N. J.	Sept. 1, '50	17	10	78
15	John R. Smead		July 1, '50	19	7	18
16	Michael R. Morgan	La.	do	17	5	
17	Stephen D. Lee	S. C.	do	16	9	67
18	Milton T. Carr	Va.	do	17	10	10
19	William D. Pender	N. C.	do	16	4	18
20	Loomis L. Langdon	N. Y.	do	19	8	100
21	John T. Greble	Pa.	do	16	5	64
22	John B. Villepigue	S. C.	do	19	11	13
23	Henry A. Smalley	Vt.	do	16	4	67
24	Samuel Kinsey	Pa.	do	16	11	55
25	Abner Smead	Ga.	do	17	3	87
26	Oliver B. Greene	N. Y.	July 1, '49	16	6	99
27	Stephen H. Weed	N. Y.	July 1, '50	18	7	97
28	E. Franklin Townsend	Wis.	Sept. 1, '50	17	1	66
29	Alfred B. Chapman	Ala.	do	20	11	16
30	George A. Gordon	At Large	July 1, '50	17	0	66
31	John O. Long	At Large	do		8	84
32	Benjamin F. Davis	Miss.	do	18	8	97
33	James Wright	N. Y.	July 1, '49	20	2	99
34	Waterman Palmer Jr.	Pa.	July 1, '50	18	1	97
35	David P. Hancock	Pa.	July 1, '49	16	11	97

11

THIRD CLASS—57 MEMBERS—1854.

Order of general merit	Names	State	Date of admission	Age (Years)	Age (Mon)	Demerit for six months
*1	David C. Houston	N. Y.	July 1, '52	16	6	18
*2	Miles D. McAlister	Mich.	do	20	3	33
*3	George W. Snyder	N. Y.	Sept. 1, '52	19	1	43
*4	Charles C. Lee	N. C.	July 1, '52	18	7	36
*5	A. Parker Porter	Penn.	do	17	0	10
6	Orlando M. Poe	Ohio.	Sept. 1, '52	23	5	25
7	Henry V. DeHart	At Large	July 1, '52	16	11	49
8	Guilford D. Bailey	N. Y.	do	18	9	68
9	George D. Bayard	At Large	do	16	5	68
10	Herbert A. Hascall	N. Y.	do	16	9	49
11	William Gaston	At Large	do	18	8	100
12	John B. Shinn	Ohio.	do	20	4	52
13	Edmund C. Bainbridge	At Large	do	17	8	59
14	Hylan B. Lyon	Ky.	do	16	5	19
15	James P. Major	Mo.	do	16	1	40
16	Joseph H. Taylor	At Large	do	16	5	86
17	Lorenzo Lorain	Penn.	do	20	11	61
18	Wesley Owens	Ohio.	do	19	9	25
19	William B. Hughes	Tenn.	do	19	8	43
20	Richard Lodor	N. J.	do	19	9	32
21	Thomas W. Walker	At Large	do	19	0	36
22	James W. Forsyth	Ohio.	July 1, '51	16	9	47
23	John F. Ritter	Penn.	July 1, '52	16	5	26
24	John Bennett	Ohio.	do	18	0	39
25	George Jackson	Va.	do	19	1	49
26	Herman Biggs	Ia.	do	19	1	32
27	Thomas C. Sullivan	Ohio.	July 1, '52	18	6	42
28	John K. Mizner	Mich.	do	18	4	56
29	Jeremiah H. Gilman	Me.	do	20	7	15
30	Thomas E. Miller	Ky.	do	16	5	44
31	John Tipton	Ia.	do	19	2	44
32	Lunsford L. Lomax	At Large	do	16	2	66
33	John W. Barriger	Ky.	Sept. 1, '52	20	1	29
34	William H. Jackson	Tenn.	July 1, '51	16	9	35
35	James McMillan	N. Y.	do	20	3	38

18

CONDUCT ROLL—1854.

Number	Names	Class	Demerit for the year	Number	Names	Class	Demerit for the year
73	William R. Pease	2	102	109	William T. Gentry	3	133
74	Thomas W. Walker	3	103	110	Thomas C. Sullivan	3	133
75	J. L. Kirby Smith	4	106	111	James H. Hill	2	134
76	Alexander S. Webb	2	106	112	James W. Forsyth	3	134
77	Herbert A. Hascall	3	107	113	John T. Mercer	1	135
78	Owen K. McLemore	3	108	114	Franck B. Armistead	3	135
79	Michael P. Small	2	110	115	Edward R. Warner	1	135
80	William D. Pender	1	111	116	David H. Brotherton	1	136
81	Ellison L. Costin	4	111	117	Israel C. Morris	3	136
82	Samuel Breck, Jr.	2	112	118	Richard H. Brewer	3	136
83	John R. Church	2	112	119	Nathaniel E. Venables	3	138
84	William R. Likens	2	114	120	Stephen D. Lee	1	139
85	John Tipton	3	116	121	John McCleary	1	139
86	George D. Bayard	3	116	122	E. Franklin Townsend	1	139
87	John F. Ritter	3	117	123	Wimer Bedford	4	139
88	Joseph B. Conrad	4	117	124	Thomas J. Berry	4	139
89	John K. Mizner	3	119	125	J. McLean Hildt	3	140
90	John T. Magruder	4	119	126	George D. Ruggles	2	142
91	John Pegram	1	129	127	John B. Shinn	3	142
92	George Jackson	3	120	128	Lunsford L. Lomax	3	143
93	John T. Greble	1	121	129	Edward J Connor	4	143
94	Thomas J. Treadwell	1	121	130	John M. McCaffrey	1	143
95	Richard Lodor	3	122	131	Charles G. Rogers	1	145
96	George Ryan	4	123	132	Andrew Jackson, Jr.	4	145
97	Timothy M. Bryan, Jr.	2	124	133	Thomas J. Lee	4	145
98	John Bennett	3	124	134	Allen A. Bursley	2	146
99	James P. Major	3	126	135	William J. A. McGrath	4	146
100	Manning M. Kimmel	4	125	136	Guilford D. Bailey	3	147
101	John V. D. DuBois	2	126	137	A. Sinclair Cunningham	3	147
102	Henry A. Smalley	1	127	138	Henry V. DeHart	3	147
103	James E. B. Stuart	1	129	139	Harrison B C. Lord	4	147
104	Ira W. Claflin	4	129	140	James McMillan	3	147
105	Paul J. Quattlebaum	4	132	141	John C. Frary	3	148
106	Horace Randal	1	133	142	Robert H. Anderson	4	148
107	William B. Hazen	2	133	143	Brayton C. Ives	4	149
108	Edmund C. Bainbridge	3	133	144	Lorenzo Lorain	3	149

*Some pages from the Official Register of Cadets of the U.S. Military Academy (1854) showing names of Custis Lee, J. E. B. Stuart, John Pegram, and others mentioned in the journal.
Courtesy of the Virginia Historical Society.*

picture above the altar. In the afternoon A & I walked to the lower church. It was very late so we almost raced, being very warm this was not pleasent. Emmie Agnel persisted in walking home with me & making Annie take her seat in the carriage. We were soon joined by two "gray coats". Now if there is anything I fairly *hate* it is to have anyone, especially a cadet, join me when walking, I willingly see them in the house but elsewhere I can't stand them. Fortunately this one was a little Virginian whom I knew as well as my own name so I didn't mind him *much*. I invited him to spend the summer at Arlington & as we went to school in the fall we could put him down at Charlottesville. In his turn he promised to fire guns to commemorate my departure next morning from reveille 'till twelve! Emmy's escort being a Virginian too I could offer to take lots of messages home for them. The whole corps promised to give us numerous vials of their tears bottled for the occasion—thus following the example of an illustrious Captain!

On returning home Maggie & Sallie came in for a little while & promised with the other girls to meet us at the wharf to say goodbye.

Then Annie & I walked out to the Cemetary. How solemn it was with all those cold white monuments around us—All the time after that the house was crowded it did not seem at all like Sunday. We talked and laughed not realizing we might never see them again. The cadets gave us a very sweet Serenade the Sat. week before we left. They played "Home sweet Home", "Carry me back to Ole Virginny" & others. We threw them boquets in grand style. The following Wed. about 9 P.M. the band gave us a splendid serenade, Mr. Apelles was then called in when he parted from his interesting pupils. Monday morning I gave a last frantic gaze at guard mounting, my last sight of a grey coat & brass button the last notes of the beautiful band. After this the house was full the whole time though it was pouring rain. Everyone was very kind. Chudie got a permit to tell us good-bye. I couldn't feel as if I was really going, I couldn't raize a tear, indeed I felt *heartless* when even the domestics were full of tears. It was not until we were all in the omnibus, until I gave a last look at our house & garden, then turned to the plain & saw it so dreary & wet, & finally caught sight of Chudie & Miss Rebecca come sadly out of our gate, under a dripping umbrella their whole air betokening desertion & sorrow that I gave & cried as if—Oh I don't know—but I felt so sad & forlorn I cried 'till my eyes were blinded. The Heavens seemed to sympathize with us, it shed torrents of tears & as we crossed the river in open boats everything was pretty well soaked. Still the wharf was crowded with umbrellas shielding officers & some few ladies to bid "a last a long farewell". Judge & Mrs. Wayne with Jimmy Cuyler went down with us. It was like meeting old friends as we jumped out of the cars to see Mr. Sackett's & Maj. Porter's[83] well known faces, they had come down in the early train to see the officers who were just going off to Europe.

We were most kindly received at Mrs. Cook's, I didn't think much of West Point until we went to bed & then I had one more good cry. We visited Mr. Cozzens' house, next morning, to see some beautiful pictures of his—from there to the Academy of Design. It was raining very hard but Sister, Helen Peters, Annie & I went on to the Chrystal Palace stopping on our way to see Mrs. G. W. Smith. We saw many beautiful things at the Palace especially the Statuary & paintings. Next morning we started for Balt. Mrs. Gen. Scott & a very pretty bride, Mrs. Halleck,[84] we met on the cars. At Phila a Mr. Ogden joined our party who was very kind to us all. From French town we traveled by water. It was the first time I had been on the Chesapeake, it was fascinating to gaze down down into the water. We had a delightful supper fresh perch was

83. Maj. Porter—Fitz-John Porter was an Instructor of Artillery and Cavalry. Porter became a major general of the U.S. Army but was cashiered.

84. Halleck—Maria DeHart (Mayo) Scott (1789–1862) and Elizabeth (Hamilton) Halleck.

so like getting home! Then I took a long nice nap for we did not reach Balt. until eleven. We four chicks being considered models of propriety were put in one carriage alone. Aunt Anne was looking very badly. She can only move her head. One foot is sprained, & she only uses one arm a little. She hasn't been out of bed since October. I think when I am tempted to complain hereafter I will remember her & cease.

Cousin Anne Carter lives next door, she has a large family & crowds of cousins now staying with them. Charlotte Wickham,[85] one of them, is not much older than I, is very pretty & sweet, & I liked her very much. We were all invited to dine at Mrs. Bonaparte's but only Pa, Ma & Mildred went. Sister remained with Aunt Anne, the rest of our party left Sat. morning for Washington.

85. Charlotte Wickham—a distant cousin of the Lees', who later married Rooney. She died during the war.

Arlington for the Summer

The summer of 1855 brought the Lees back to Arlington with West Point only a poignant memory. Lieutenant Colonel Lee had been transferred from the Corps of Engineers to the new 2nd Cavalry and was to be stationed somewhere in the West. He was sorely missed by his family, and they even more by him, but all accepted such separations as part of his career in the Army.

Agnes' descriptions of her fourteenth summer give a vivid picture of a way of life that was soon to vanish forever. In the large houses like Arlington, well staffed by slaves, there was a continuing exchange of visits and visitors of all ages. Most of the guests were related by birth or by marriage; Virginia was still an agrarian state, thinly populated. The privileged class was small and known to one another; the intermarriage of cousins was frequent.

The visit to Cedar Grove that Agnes relates in detail is typical. Four of the Arlington Lees joined more than a dozen cousins for a sojourn of almost two weeks; "there was plenty of room for us all," she writes. The sixty-mile journey was made by boat on the Potomac; there were more rivers than good roads in Virginia and waterways were the highways. At Cedar Grove visits were exchanged with other cousins at neighboring plantations. Agnes *makes it easy for us to imagine the conversation at such gatherings: "I heard the affairs of the Lees, Carters, Childes, Grymes and others discussed at length." Births, deaths, courtships, weddings, a sincere and affectionate interest in the lives of a very large family, were the warp and woof of daily living.*

[Continuing 17 April 1855]

We soon jumped into *our* carriage & after putting Pa down at the War Office started home. I felt so excited I could hardly keep still. It seemed an age before we dashed around the garden fence. I sprang out on the steps kissed Grandpa, & Cousin Markie, ran out to tell the servants how d'ye do & then wandered all over the house. But everywhere one was missing, & in the evening when my excited feelings had cooled down I wandered alone to my Grandma's grave. I kissed it over & over then knelt down & prayed to God to sustain me to make me worthy to join her in the beautiful sky above. I thought of the last morning I was at West Point, when I went into a little room knelt down on some mattresses & prayed—Oh I believe I really did almost pray then!—that Our Father in Heaven would bring us home safely, and that He would satisfy that longing within me to *do* something to *be* something. I long I don't know what for but for something to fill the void in my heart. I did feel a kind of sweet peace as I knelt there the mattresses wet with my tears & my eyes full asking that my prayers might come from my very soul that they might be *real*. But it all soon passed away & now I am as bad nay worse than ever. Will I ever be a christian? Ever be worthy of the love & esteem of anyone? O I hope so—but I am afraid not.

Dear old Mammy is very weak & thin, she must be seventy six at least, she is an old Mt. Vernon Servant & so faithful to us.

I heard from Custis Saturday, he was then at St. Mary's but must have reached Amelia Island ere this. Papa leaves for Louisville[86] to-morrow I am *so sorry*. But *I am so tired* I must stop.

20th.

Papa left us Wed. He hopes to return in a month. I answered Custis's letter yesterday—long & most stupidly. In it I mention "Mon journal precieux" which I told him I knew he would like to read—but No! it is only intended for my edification, mine alone. I have been reading Lady Willoughby's diary, it is very simple & sweet. Mine could certainly be improved by taking hers as a model but no—bad as it is it is original to myself. Here I scratch off whatever first comes to my mind, so it would never bear criticism from another less partial critic.

I have been gardening & planting many flowers. It is very very warm. Brunetta has nine fine little chicks. None of the boxes have yet arrived from West Point. I declare I hardly like to think of that charming "spot of earth now—I had no idea I would regret leaving it so much but when I reflect I will probably never be there again—at least until the place & people are entirely changed it is perfectly mournful. Just think of Flirtation walk! the beautiful Hudson lashing those grand old rocks, the bright-green plain, the parades, the music—everything! O how often in the clear early mornings have I heard the solemn strains of that exquisite German hymn come streaming in through the closed blinds & have thrown them wide to catch every note. The concerts all seem beautiful now. If I could only hear the band *once* more.

When we first left, I used to feel if I could go back for one day just to tread the side walk once more, to swing open our gate & see one familiar face how delightful it would be. I was always

---

86. Louisville—one of the stops on the way to St. Louis, where the 2nd Cavalry was training.

saying to Annie or myself Now they are going to dinner!; now the bugle for—is blowing (oh those beautiful bugles!) now is parade time—now the gun fires—now tatoo is beating, or there is guard-mounting, or we ought to be going round to french, or this is Mr. Apelles' morning—every hour of the day had some association.

But I am very happy here my dear old home that has *always* been my home—not a two year sojourn! West Point is probably more striking & picturesque, but Arlington with its commanding view, fine old trees, and the soft wild luxuriance of its woods can favorably compare with any home I've seen!

23rd.

This is the anniversary of my precious Grandmamma's death. Two years ago how I felt my first real grief. O that terrible Saturday. I would not, could not believe the heart that had always been so faithful & loving had ceased to beat. How vividly it all comes back to me.

27th.

I have just finished the 1st Vol. of Irving's 'Columbus.' It is beautiful. Just think how long he had to wait to discover a world! If he had only known it was not Asia but an entirely new continent, that another and broader ocean lay between the land of his discovery and the continent he had left. I noticed when the Spaniards came to the island they saw the first use of the tobacco plant. 'Tis a pity as they thought it so nauseous then it could not have been exterminated, for really seeing some one I had known at W.P. loafing along in Washington a segar in his mouth etc. conveying the idea of such a perfect rowdy disgusted me more than ever with its use. If I were "Queen of these United States" not one plant should remain in the country any hour.

May 13th.

This beautiful bright Sunday morning I am seated at my desk writing. How my thoughts should rise to the Great Creator who gave it to us. We have not gone to church this morning but I have just returned from prayers. In the evening we have a meeting house, held chiefly for the servants to attend. It is about a mile from the house. After that a doz. or more little children of the sable race come up to say their hymns etc. Last Wed. Ma, Mildred & I spent the day at Cameron, Smith, Dan M—— & Rob. were there. Uncle Smith[87] has just returned from the Japan Expedition, with lots of boxes filled with pretty things. He gave each of us a pretty poena dress, Mamma a japanese waiter & each of us girls a lacca workbox. Our Rob. has a curious chinese kite.

I have now almost finished the 3rd vol. of Columbus. His last days were the saddest of all Ferdinand's treatment was unbearable, I felt—I hardly know how—but only wished I had been a *man* then! Columbus should have found out he had *one* friend in the world. But 'tis all past now.—

20th.

We are very busy all the time now cleaning, fixing, working hard to renovate our dear old home. Aunt Nannie, Uncle S—— & Robert C—— arrived during the confusion to spend a few days. Rob. is the sweetest little monkey I ever saw. The Jasmine is almost gone, I am so sorry, it is one of my "ambitions" to visit the places where Jasmine grows wild all through the woods. Cousin Markie is soon going to Buffalo. Mamma, Annie, Rob. & I are going to Cedar Grove[88] next Wednesday. I am busy now teaching Marcelina be-

---

87. Uncle Smith—Sidney Smith Lee (1802–1869), brother of Robert E. Lee, commanded the *Princeton* on Commodore Perry's trip to Japan.
88. Cedar Grove—King George County home of Dr. Richard Stuart, whose wife was a cousin of Mrs. Lee.

fore breakfast & Emma, afterwards—besides there are my Sunday scholars so I am both a pupil & Mistress.

Mamma has heard from Cousin Marietta that Ida is going to be married the 6th June. I fear she is too lovely a girl for him, but I trust her influence will work for his good. Yesterday a most mysterious little roll arrived from the office for Miss Annie Lee. On opening we found two graduating songs sent to herself & myself by Messrs. Dick & Wheeler, of course I was charmed to find my "Valentine" had not forgotten me.

June 8th.

We have been & returned from C.G. which is more than sixty miles down the river. We started, with Mr. Webster in the "Columbia" which literally *pokes*, found on board Cousin Eugenia Hall,[89] & Alice Bowie with their children, & Ella Carter,[90] who were going with us also Cousin Roberta Stuart & Sarah en route for "Panorama" a few miles from the Stuarts.

11th.

I was interrupted last Friday & shall endeavour to continue though I am suffering from inflamed eyes which warn me to be careful. Pa is here for only one week, it is too bad! We are expecting Mrs. Cook, & Miss Helen also Mrs. Barnes, Mitty Randolph & perhaps Rebecca Sprole. Then the graduates will soon be set free & many were the visits promised after that. —but I must continue the account of our late visit. After becoming perfectly worn out we at last reached "Boyd's hole" about one, & were transported to the shore in row boats. There in the burning sun we waited until our

89. Cousin Eugenia Hall—Eugenia Calvert (Carter) Hall.
90. Ella Carter—Ella (Carter) George.

belongings were safely deposited, & then drove to the house, Annie & I with the nurses & two babies in the wagon. I had "Robert Grahame" which I *screamed* to Annie, amidst the noise & jolting of our vehicle. The portico was filled with a mass of pink robed females & I assure you it was with no little dread I anticipated my introduction to my unknown cousins. We sprang out, kissed them all promiscously & were conducted hot & tired to our rooms. It is one of the most convenient houses I ever saw. A fine hall, with dining room & sitting-room one side from which you pass to the wing containing the office pantries etc; the other side the parlour, staircase, library etc.—altogether some eleven or twelve bedrooms. One hall door opens on the river about twenty yards distant, it is nearly five miles wide just opposite. Every one was so affectionate & kind, Margaret & Julia were at school in Balt., but the Dr., Cousin L——, Rosalie, the eldest daughter, who is very sweet & pretty, Mary Ada,[91] Carrie, little Dick & Calvert, Cousin Julia Morris, the Halls, Bowies, Ella & Mildred C—— & ourselves composed a large household, but there was plenty of room for all. I shan't be able to describe half the pleasures of our visit. The first Saturday most of our party went to spend the day with Cousin Patsy Stuart, who lives a few miles down the river. Many of us walked from the shore & stopped at Mr. Tenant's to see a pretty view but I haven't seen anything that competes with that from Arlington yet. We found "quite a company" awaiting us, & every thing was done to make us enjoy ourselves, not forgetting a fine dinner at which a roast pig with an apple in his mouth was eminently conspicuous. I never saw anything like the beautiful roses in King George, they are in the greatest profusion at Liberty. We had a charming row home, the tide was so low the boatmen

91. Margaret—Margaret (Stuart) Hunter (1837–1893), Julia Calvert (Stuart) Jones, Rosalie Eugenia (Stuart) Stuart (1835–1915), Ada (Stuart) Randolph Robb (1841–1914).

had to bear us ashore in their arms. "Joshua" was my bearer "Moses", Annie's. The funniest thing was to see Dr. Stuart who is very tall, on the back of one of the shortest men carried safely to land. Rob, Dick & Calvert waded of course. The next week the girls had to say their lessons to Miss Taborah still we had a nice time. One day Mamma, Cousin Julia, & I went round returning visits, I heard the affairs of the Lees, Carters, Childes, *Grymes & others* discussed at length. At Mrs. Grymes we saw her daughter Mrs. Tolivar, who has nine children living all girls except one. The eldest I saw was nine years old the youngest a baby. All of the others seem just the same size. What a tribe for one poor woman! One Wed. the elders spent the day with Cousin Margaret Lomax, we children joined them in the evening gaining a *wagon* ride. We had a charming evening. Mr. Webster was there! It was amusing everywhere to see the dearth of *beaux*; though almost all that could be collected were at Panarama. They little knew with what condescension I, who had been accustomed to the elite of W.P. & in such numbers too, privately looked down upon their attentions!

We went in bathing by moonlight several times, it was *perfectly* delightful. We feasted on crabs, fried chickens, green peas, cake strawberries & ice cream which latter was particularly acceptable. Cousin Eugenia has two beautiful little boys; Alice's are not so pretty nor *so* bad, but she is lovely, the prettiest of the family. Sat. notwithstanding a pouring rain we started for Boyd's hole & after waiting *four bonafidae* hours for the "Alice Rice" we had to turn back. It was provoking after all the trouble & waiting, though we were very glad to see them again. The Columbia bore us safely to Alexa next day. I engaged to take care of Carter in the boat, I can tell I had a time of it. Such restlessness it makes me tired to think of it. We found Mildred waiting for us at Aunt Rosalie's with any no. of letters from Papa, Custis, Sister, Mrs. Symington, Mrs. Dick Smith, Miss Susan P——, Neva & Cadet Stuart that was. I was amused at the different parts of the U.S. from which they came.

Grandpa was in dispair of our ever returning though we hadn't been gone two weeks. Yesterday a pair of new carriage horses were purchased. "Lion" gave out about a week ago, so Grandpapa who is always prompt in this particular sent far & wide for a successor & these two are chosen instead of Tiger & the King of beasts. Miss Helen Peters has arrived alone, Mrs. Cook is to follow her next week. Helen's tongue goes as fast as ever!

July 8th.

We have a house full of company, Mrs. Cook, little Arthur & Annie, Helen, Ella Carter & our last arrivals of yesterday—Mrs. Barnes, Joe & Anna. It was charming to see a *West-Point* face again. That "land of dear delight" seems to have become a dream of the past. I wonder I used to think it so monotonous. Last Friday before breakfast Annie & I respectively on Anne & Santa Anna[92] with Old Dan'l astride Grace made our way to Warwick. We had a nice visit & our ride home was charming, little Santie galloped splendidly. O I have forgotten to say anything about the "glorious fourth." Grandpa attended the celebration in W—— & it *poured* almost the whole time. After tea there was a grand display on the Arlington Portico—of cushions shawls etc. to make us comfortable while gazing at the magnificent fireworks which were to astonish the millions. Well we waited and waited, one or two faint efforts were made but it was "no go" & we went in—much scandalized by the idea of a "4th" without fireworks. Hopes were held out for the next night another preparation—another failure. "They were wet—they would be ready by Saturday." A third effort to see what was not to be & we gave up. Just to think! the first class have graduated. One extremely *hot* morning as I was sending forth

---

92. Santa Anna—a pony Lee shipped back from Mexico for the children. Grace (Darling) had been Lee's own horse in Mexico.

sweet strains in the shape of five finger exercises, a stylish gig drove up, of course I made my "depart" but not before staring Mr. Hetzel in the face through the open window. What was my consternation to be commanded to return at once to the apartment I had so unceremoniously quit as the only one at all presentable. There was Mr. H—— & Mr. Wheeler. I don't know why or wherefore but I felt so frightened all the time, that though I was crazy to hear something of the Point, I could scarcely have a *tolerable* time. Presently another vehicle appeared with two other 'messieurs', I only felt 'I must go' & without a second thought I vanished into the wing. My next appearance was at dinner. Cadets (or Lieuts.) Reno & Thomas were presented. Mr. W—— was so *juvenile* he came on the childrens' side of the table where he made himself as absurdly amusing to Mildred & me as usual—his pathetic speeches being slightly inconsistent with his fine appetite.

Mrs. G. W. has been at West Point, 'twas said left for this place but she has not arrived. Church & Nichols have gone to Canada what for no one knows. But the most interesting piece of news is Mr. Casey[93] & Emma Wier are to be married in May! Mr. C—— has just been left by an Uncle $30,000. I am always delighted to hear of "the Army" receiving wealth, & it is particularly fortunate for a 2nd Lt. about to enter matrimony. Here is another marriage. Cousin Emma Randolph to Mr. Stark—next Tuesday. He is neither young nor handsome but well off—& I sincerely hope will prove all she wishes. Mrs. Barnes has given Sister a pretty cameo breastpin, Mamma a lace collar—& one to Annie & me. She is very sweet & kind—what a pity she is deaf. Rebecca Sprole was expected with her but did not come. Grandpa has given Sister, Annie, & me jet necklaces & bracelets they are pretty but rather useless. Aunt Nannie, little Rob & perhaps Uncle Smith have gone to W.P. how charming to have been of the party.

93. Casey—Thomas Lincoln Casey (1831–1896).

July ——

With eyes half open I shall attempt to write a few lines. Not long ago I was in a delightful dose covered with papers to keep off the flies, when a rap at the door collected my dreaming senses sufficiently to jump up. It was Julia wanted something for Mrs. Barnes. Then there was to go in the store room etc. until I was completely aroused. A second attempt to put myself in the same blissful condition was unsuccessful. Yesterday eve. Ma. Sister Miss Helen & Mrs. B—— went over to the President's grounds to hear the music. While gone a buggy drove up in which was seated Mr. Peet. Mrs. Cook was on the steps and received him though a stranger to her. Presently Perry knocked & said Mr. P—— wanted to see me. I could not believe it, but robed & went out. He came to spend the night & have meeting this evening. Ella Carter has looked lovely the whole of her stay almost as pretty as Alice did at Cedar Grove. Last Wed. they were all at the Capitol grounds when Ella's brother Bernard arrived to carry home. He is quite handsome though not as much so as I had heard. The other morning Joe & I were sent to the farm on a message. Ann was my charger, Santy his. We had almost reached the first gate when it commenced to "pour". Like geese we turned back, it stopped & it again turned. After passing through the two gates & a large drove of cattle my comb took it into its head to fall, I thinking *Ann* would never move jumped off & ran back to pick it up. But as I came up to her she started off just fast enough to prevent my catching so I had the pleasure of running all of the rest of the way. Joe in the meantime who was before commenced to scream out "catch that horse up there." When I reached the old ox house little Austin stood holding my quiet charger & Uncle Charles & Austin gazing at me in the wildest alarm. I professed, as I felt great unconcern & jumping on a cart mounted, but what was my amusement on looking over the fence to see some thirty ebony faces, the overseer at their head, staring at me with the utmost curiosity & consternation. I could scarcely contain myself. Of course they thought I had been thrown; but I do not wonder my appearance startled them, there I sat, my hair streaming down my back, my hat bent in every direction by the rain suspended from my shoulders, my riding skirt wet & my face brilliant with my race—altogether a comical object.

Sept. 2nd.

I must write a little today for I have not for six weeks. A great many events have taken place but first I must say I am writing in the 'big room' now the parlour. The carpenters the masons, the plasterers, the painters have left at last & lo! the change they have wrought.[94] The white walls adorned with fine pictures in gilded frames, the marble mantels, white bolts & woodwork, the dark walnut doors the register of a furnace everything combined denote a change. Well do I remember the old brick walls thickly & most confusedly covered with dusky pictures half unframed, the thick rafters above fit harbingers for cobwebs & dust, the rusty brass bolts, unpolished doors & unpainted wood, while three venerable presses from Mt. Vernon filled with old & mouldy books, a half broken table, an ancient harpsichord & several wooden chairs formed the prominent portion of the furniture. Many *&* many a time in our childish days of course, have we ridden round & round on stick horses making stables of the niches in the Arches, & behind the old pictures, and making houses of vast extent with the old furniture. If these scenes are ever to be reenacted as the Indians retreat farther West, we will be driven to the painting room & the various "cloisters" beyond. We have sent for our furniture at W.P.; then velvet & marble will fill this apartment, parisien clocks will tingle their silvery bells from the mantels, crystal chandeliers on golden brackets will shed their soft light

---

94. Arlington renovation—Some rooms of the house had never been finished.

from the walls, handsome cases with well bound & titled books, & rare curiosities will display their treasures & the sound of gay music & dancing, with merry laughter can complete the picture. What a brilliant room. I have conjured up, though I commenced my description in fun I have not deviated from facts. The hall has been rewashed & the pictures so nicely hung. Sister is making frames ornamented with leather for Grandpa's pictures; hung up high they look very well.[95] Our old parlours are now the dining-room. All this time our dear Papa is at Jefferson Barracks, far away from those he loves it is too bad. Rooney has spent his six weeks vacation from Cambridge with us. Rebecca returned North with him. A great many of the Cedar Grove Stuarts have been here from time to time. We are going to Staunton in ten days just think of it! Mary & Ada Stuart & Annette Carter are going with us. We are very busy getting ready. I must stop, leaving an important event (Mr. Wheeler's engagement!) for another time.

95. Grandpa's pictures—Custis was an avid painter of Revolutionary scenes, Indians, and wildlife.

Staunton

In September 1855 Annie and Agnes entered the Virginia Female Institute in Staunton, a relatively new school for girls that was under the auspices of the Episcopal Diocese of Virginia.

By reading the following paragraphs taken from an 1876 catalogue of the Virginia Female Institute one can easily realize that, though the prices quoted would bring joy to a present-day parent's heart, today's student would not be enthusiastic about a boarding school of the 1850's.

BUILDINGS

The Building was designed by a skillful Architect and in 1846 was erected and furnished in handsome style at an expense of more than fifteen thousand dollars. Its dormitories, designed for four pupils to each are large & airy and can comfortably accomodate sixty Boarders. The grounds embrace four acres and are improved with firm gravel walks, shrubbery and shade trees.

Journal of Agnes Lee

CHARGES—PER ANNUAL SESSION

The charge for board (including furnished room & use of bedding) washing, fuel, light and tuition in the English house is $200.00

Extra Charges, per Annual Session

Music:	Piano and Organ, with use of instruments—	
	each	60.00
	Guitar	50.00
	Harp, and Use of Instrument	80.00
Languages: Latin, Greek, French, Spanish and Italian—		
each		20.00
Drawing and Painting		20.00
Sacred Music, a general daily exercise		5.00
Vocal Music		50.00
Pew Rent		2.50

DAILY EXERCISES

Three quarters of an hour after the rising bell, the Boarders assemble with an Officer, for the silent study of the Scriptures. At a specified hour after breakfast all pupils are assembled in the Study Hall for worship of which Sacred music, accompanied with an instrument and under the direction of a Professor, forms an interesting part. A precept and promise previously selected from the Bible are repeated by the pupils and after worship they are dismissed, in sections, to their respective recitation rooms.

Parents should specify the epistolary correspondents of the pupils and inform the Principal in general terms as to the visits they may make and the calls they may receive.

The calls of gentlemen who may be strangers to the Principal and not specified by the parents are not received by the pupils unless authorized by letters of introduction. From 4 o'clock to 5 P.M., is the most convenient hour for such calls.

Pupils will not be allowed to receive calls on the Sabbath unless under very extraordinary circumstances.

Pupils will not be allowed, *under any circumstances*, to spend the night out of the Institute.

An advertisement for the school declares that "The Institute is strictly first class *and with a very large* first class *patronage from all the Southern States."*

Staunton, March 16th 1856.

Yes, "Mr. Wheeler's engagement was postponed for another time —for a time when it must be chronicled as his "marriage." How absurd such an idea would have seemed last winter, yet it was actually last winter the affair was arranged—and by letter too.

But I certainly forget I am a school girl an inmate of the so called "Staunton Jail." On the 12th of last Sept. 1855 the whole Stuart family, Cousin Charles Carter, Annette, Sister, Annie & I, after a tiresome journey arrived in Staunton. After dinner at the Va. hotel, the five school girls attended by their afflicted relatives wended their way up to the Institute. Mr. & Mrs. Sheffey[96] received the whole party with many smiles, *at last* distinguished the scholars & we were immured. I believe we all cried a little & refused to go down to tea, upon its being brought up to Mary, she exclaimed "O girls it is sweetened with *brown* sugar!" which restored our drooping spirits. Our relatives staid several days expecting to go to Weyer's cave but the weather prevented. Monday they left O *how* we felt it! I have no time to tell my first

96. Mrs. and Mrs. Sheffey—Mrs. Sheffey had run a small school which became the Virginia Female Institute, but her relationship to the school at this time is unclear.

The Virginia Female Institute in Staunton (described by Agnes as the "Staunton Jail") as it was in 1855. The building is now part of Stuart Hall. Courtesy of Stuart Hall.

impressions. Mr. Phillips[97] is handsome and attractive but I am still not so perfectly fascinated as most of the girls. Mr. Wheat[98] I like very much. He is smart & intelligent, besides very funny—but *no* beauty. Mr. Sheffey is a particular little man, Mrs. S—— very sweet & kind but makes you feel she can be very severe. Miss Beckely is our cousin pretty & sweet, but quite strict & rather cold. Mr. de Rinzie is very leinient, so odd & ———. Mr. Engelbrecht, our music teacher, is a very good one, we all like him. Mr. Cole-man, our drawing master is the only *young* man & his class is a privileged one. I suppose they think his looks will prevent our being very desperate. These are my teachers now for the girls, what seventy five of them? & many day schollars too. I like them generally very well. We five are to-gether in a large room. Are

97. Mr. Phillips—The Rev. Mr. R. H. Phillips was headmaster of the Institute.
98. Mr. Wheat—The Rev. Mr. James C. Wheat, Assistant Principal of the school.

known as "the five cousins" & are led to consider ourselves "something." We all went to our homes for Christmas. Papa was there all the time. He is now in Texas O so far away he seems. I love him so much. We hear from home every week the letters are treasures. Now we do nothing but study & look forward to next summer with *so* much pleasure, counting the days to our departure with great zeal. Sister is going to Balt. & Helen P. who has been staying at home accompanies her that far. Rooney spent his vacation at home had a charming time. He & Mary were a good deal in Washington with Ella & Margaret. I suppose they had fine times at the parties etc. Rob is going to school at Mr. Lippitts. But I must really go to bed for we are no sluggards here but rise between four & five o'clock.

March 11th.

I must write a little tonight though I feel miserably. This is "blue Monday" & it has been *blue* to me. We are to be examined in Arithmetic on Wed. I never have been examined & dread it. We had a great deal of fun this eve. in drawing class & then up here. We burnt a piece of bristol board took the ashes & gave ourselves ferocious moustaches & eyebrows. A great many of the girls came to view the four young gentlemen for Mary was taking her music lesson. Her first exclamation on returning was, "do girls clean up your faces, but the 2nd gong sounded so down Annette & I marched to supper. We were told Mrs. Sheffey would "censure" us so I seized my handkerchief, & quickly caused what "Drusy" called my *whiskers* to vanish. She didn't come to tea so our trouble was for nothing. The girls were much amused even the dim similitude to a masculine in the V.F.I. caused great disturbance.

March 21st.

I must try to write a few lines tonight merely to inform—I don't know who—that we are to have holiday until next Tuesday! One of the precious days has passed it is Friday night—Good Friday. O when I think this day so many years ago Our blessed Savior died it impresses me with an awful feeling. Yet I spent the day most carelessly, as if I had never had a Saviour to die for me. I cannot say that for I have thought of Him several times, but my foot being sore I could not go to church, & when the girls returned I commenced to read aloud to Ada a book called Madeline. I read as fast as I could with scarcely a moments interruption until after tea & finished it, it is quite a thick book. It is a journal kept by the heroine herself, the "history of a *weak* woman's heart" she says.

Sunday morn. 23rd.

This is Easter Sunday the day on which our blessed Lord arose. I can't go to Church on account of my feet, when will they be well? In addition my finger is rising, how it pains & burns. It kept me awake last night—so I feel miserably. The girls have all gone to church so alone, home sick & in pain I must pour out my sad thoughts to my journal as Madeline used to do. I love that book. She was so beautiful, so noble, & so devoted to him who had the love of her whole heart. But why I am so miserable I can't fine out. I am not in love certainly, had I every disposition I should like to see the one, who could win ones heart in Staunton that I've seen. I only know I want to go home O so much! & I want to go to West Point. I feel half crazy to go there this morning, & will I ever? No, never,—until at least I am changed, those I care for are gone, & the very place, whose every stone I so vividly remember, won't be the same. If I could only fly there this Sunday, & go to church in our chapel again. Why can't I tread those dear old side walks once more, & enter what I once called that ugly *wooden* house. And then the band, O I so often *long* to hear it, I believe "Home sweet Home" would set me wild! What makes me love the place so? I don't know nor care, I only feel I *must* be there I could almost kiss the ground I have so carelessly trodden upon. I hardly know why my thoughts so often turn back to the two happy winters I spent there, sometimes with an irresistable (longing) to bring them back again. Those were such dreamy days of thoughtlessness & pleasure, I can scarcely believe a place so beautiful with both nature & art was so short a time ago my home. I wonder how I ever could have wished to leave it. It seems so far away now. How happy we were, how we laughed & idled our time with thoughtless gaiety. How silly I was then! & how silly now, I almost believe I am losing my senses to write in this way. But I have such longings sometimes, such *yearnings* for something I know not what. Is it to be loved, to be worshiped by something or some one—No—that is *sinful*, silly & impossible. I hope, I pray my *yearnings* my "streachings into the unseen"—the unknown may be for something holier higher than I have yet felt—That I may know what true satisfaction, true peace is. I am told & I know I can, I must find it in the bosom of my Saviour & only there. I have tried, but my heart seems shut up, it is so hard! it will not receive lasting impressions, I have often determined to try to be a christian, I have thought I had asked Aid from Above, but in a day everything good has vanished. Sometimes the awful thought comes to me, I am one of those who are never to be good—one of the doomed. If any one hereafter should see what I have here written, they must not judge me too harshly, if they could only feel as I feel sometimes—& now they would pity me. I am generally thought—I feel—bright & gay as other girls are, but I confess there are times when I feel scarcely sensible, when my poor weak, miserable nature makes me despise myself with a force which no language of mine can describe, then every slight, every sarcasm, every neglect seems to go my very heart almost to breaking. Then I wish I couldn't think that I was plunged from day to day in something that would absorb me entirely, but no, it would be too dreadful so, if I couldn't *think* a second life would be taken from me. O may a time come for me, weak & wicked as I am, when I may be perfectly happy. But I *won't* write this way any longer, I fear this must be day-dreaming which if longer indulged in will do me harm—. I received a letter from Mamma Friday, little Fannie Cook is dead. There is something so sweet in thinking of another little angel spirit in Heaven. Several of Custis's classmates are no more. Shepperd, Davant, Palmer, Morgan, & one or two others will never again be seen by their comrades "here below." Mr. Davant was drowned while crossing the El Passo, when it was very much swollen by a flood, he was a splendid rider, & I suppose thought he was stronger than those strong waves. I can almost see him now, the morning after he graduated, when he came to say good-bye, so joyous so strong. My darling Papa is in Texas, I must write to him tomorrow. I did little else except write & practice yesterday there was so much fuss attending the preparations for our fancy ball, which I will describe another day. O my journal I hope no eyes will ever see you save mine, they only will excuse my follies & my weakness.

I had forgotten that during the time my journal was discontinued, dear old Mammy died about seventy-eight years old. One morning before Christmas, when Sister went to carry her julip she was cold & lifeless, but O I trust her spirit is in Heaven. She was as faithful as could be. How I missed her Christmas. When we paid the servants our usual visits there was one pair of steep steps up which I had no cause to go. She is the last but two of the Mt. Vernon servants. What tales she could tell of "those good old times" of Mrs. Washington's beauty & good management. How "she was one of the out-door gals & would run to open the gate for the Gen." And when my beautiful Aunt Lewis was married "how ole Mistis let all the servants come in to see it & gave them such

good things to eat," "how Ole Mistis was dressed so splendid, in a
light flowered satin your Aunt Lewis all in something white, beautiful too." But though a celebrated beauty she did not come up to
"Ole Mistis" in Mammy's eyes! she could not see why so much fuss
was made over "the genl, he was only a man!", a very good master
she was sure, but she didn't suppose he was so much better than
anyone else." O those nice talks! we won't have any more. Tomorrow will be our last day of holiday. We are to commence
Algebra & Geometry both at once, are to study hard so we may
have a *real senior* class next year. Uncle Smith is commanding at
the Phila. Navy Yard, Uncle Carter is living at a place called Wind-
sor on the James. Louis Marshall married some time ago a Miss
Florence Murray Burke from Ft. Washita, & has a son named after
his Godfather to whom they are all devoted.

Sunday night.

It is almost time for the girls to come home from Church—even
now I hear their tramping on the stairs but shall not mind them.
Nannie Smith has just left me; we have been talking & laughing
about "cher" W—— P—— & the fascinating young cadets & officers of that enchanting spot. My poor finger hurts me so I can
hardly keep still. I have written to-day to my precious Papa. Mary
Pendleton's father lectured here two weeks ago, the first lecture
on the Philosophy of dress. The ladies farthingales, little caps &
low neck dresses were well cut up amid the deafening applause of
the other sex. But our hour of triumph came, the speaker suddenly turned upon "the usurped shawl, long hair, clothes of many
colours, cuts, & styles, little patches of beard" etc. of the lords of
creation.

March 27th.

I am determined to scratch some of my foolishness this Thursday night. Mr. Everett lectured last Tuesday in Charlottesville on "Washington." Mrs. Phillips, *Harriette*, Mr. Coleman, & others went to hear him. I wish some of us poor Institutes could have escaped to the University Hall but our teachers wisely thought so many students would be overpowering. An invitation arrived this evening "for the prettiest young lady in the Institute." doubtless the young men thought it would create as much contention as the golden apple! Our first fancy ball was followed by a much better one on Monday so I shall say but little of it. The best characters were Lucie Pryor, as a corsair, Octavia Gant, an Indian, Caroline Stalnaker, a chinese, Lizzie Masters, a Kate some one & Fannie Lockhart her lover.

Sunday night my finger was so painful I did not sleep an hour but tossed in bed almost in tears, finally sprang up lighted the candle & found it ten minutes of *twelve*, when I hoped it was almost morning. I read my bible until *Monday*, then poured over Madeline to forget my pain—for at least two hours until I almost read it through again. I wish Madeline was a real character I am sure I should have loved her. I have never read a book which has taken such hold of my heart & imagination before. Perhaps it is I love to read so much & this has like such a *refreshment* among all my Philosophies & Ologies generally—. Monday eve. we received such a precious letter from Papa. It was full of strong affection. Can I ever love my parents sufficiently or repay in any measure what I owe them! That night we had quite a grand fancy ball. Josephine Stevenson & Isadore Preston were, I think the two handsomest, the former William Wallace, I—— Lady Mary. Josephine was "splendid" I quite lost my heart. A cap with black feathers, a black jacket, plaid shirt & trousers ditto, with a red scarf tied gracefully over her shoulders, made a tall & romantic looking young highlander. Before going up stairs I threw my arms round her & said I must have a kiss for she had fascinated me so I could not keep my eyes off her, as she bent her head in ready assent her romantic face & dreamy eyes were a picture to gaze upon, and if really of the other sex, I suppose to *think* upon. Lucie P—— personated Byron at fourteen—very good. Mary Pegram was Anne of Denmark, Sallie a tyrolene. Mary Burne looked sweetly as Rowena, & Rosa was in a complete man's suit. Lucie Tarry looked lovely. Caroline S—— was a green horn from the country with a *tremendous* hat, while Corrie H—— was his ever watchful spouse, sporting a straw bonnet with twenty different coloured ribbons. Under the soubriquet of Pete & Sal they amused us greatly. Sue Leith was sweetly arrayed as a flower girl. I have been very minute—more to remember the names of some of schoolmates in after years.

Sat. Night.

We had a public soiree last night. Our first french class spoke as usual, my scene contained Miss A. Lee, Lucie Pryor, Nannie, Argyle, Annette & Mary. Annie also played, Ada & I each read a composition. It was my first attempt so I was frightened. My share in the performance over, I entered the school room's back door & took my seat between Bec Wilmer & Decca Urquhart. I read Decca's journal it was chiefly filled with the praises of her idol Sue. I think Sue M—— is such a strange girl. She reminds me of Mrs. G. W. The latter found her victims among the young men while Sue is now compelled to enchant only schoolgirls. You can hardly help liking her, she has such sweet fascinating manners, she flatters you by being attentive to you. But I pity the girl who blindly loves her & tells her so, in a short time the once devoted Sue quarrels and casts her off for some new worshipper. Decca is now wrapt up in her. I only hope Sue has a heart (which she is accused of *not* having) & will not throw away Beccie's absorbing though silly affection.

14   VIRGINIA FEMALE INSTITUTE.

Miss ANNETTE CARTER,	PRINCE GEORGE'S CO., MD.
" MARY CARTER,	" " "
" SUSAN B. COCKE,	PORTSMOUTH, VA.
" ANNIE T. COCKE,	" "
" V. F. CHURCHMAN,	AUGUSTA COUNTY, VA.
" F. C. CHURCHMAN,	" " "
" E. CRUTCHFIELD,	SPOTTSYLVANIA CO. "
" ELIZABETH R. DILLARD,	HENRY COUNTY, VA.
" E. VIRGINIA DOYAL,	ASCENSION PARISH, LA.
" LUCY T. EUSTACE,	SPOTTSYLVANIA CO., VA.
" SUSAN A. FIELD,	DINWIDDIE CO., "
" J. L. FORREST,	STAUNTON, "
" N. T. FORREST,	" "
" LOUISE N. FUNSTEN,	CLARKE COUNTY, "
" OCTAVIA GANTT,	ALBEMARLE " "
" CELESTINE L. GORDON,	STAFFORD " "
" M. L. GOODWIN,	SOUTHAMPTON CO. "
" C. C. HARRISON,	LEESBURG, "
" EMMA J. HERNDON,	GREENE CO., ALA.
" M. J. JESSE,	LANCASTER COUNTY, VA.
" JULIA JESSE,	" " "
" LIZZIE L. KRATZER,	ROCKINGHAM " "
" SARAH H. KINNEY,	STAUNTON, "
" ELLEN H. KINNEY,	LEE CO., IOWA.
" ELIZABETH C. KINNEY,	LEXINGTON, KY.
" ANNA C. LEE,	ALEXANDRIA, VA.
" AGNES LEE,	" "
" CHARLOTTE T. LEWIS,	ROCKINGHAM CO., VA.
" FANNIE LOCKERT,	NORFOLK, "
" LAURA V. LORENTZ,	LOUDON CO., "
" LIZZIE E. LUCKETT,	PARISH OF RAPIDES, LA.
" MARY A. LUSHBAUGH,	STAUNTON, VA.

Partial list of students at the Virginia Female Institute showing
Annie's and Agnes' names.
Courtesy of Stuart Hall
(from Register of Officers and Pupils of Virginia Female Institute).

Sat. eve. April 6th.

I *can't* study to-night. Geometry is "Greek" or worse but indeed I feel as if I can't write either. We have had some interesting experiments in Phil. this week. I wrote a long letter to Custis today which I hope will call forth an answer as our whole family have become miserable correspondents. I give up!—

11th.

Well pauvre negligé I have only time to write five lines or more. We have had a long letter from Cousin M—— & one from Mamma. We are to dine at Boc. Chapman's tomorrow it is our first debut— from the Ins. walls so we feel quite overcome!

Sunday.

I feel tired discontented & *mad* so little disposed for writing but here sitting on the bed my book on my knee I will try. O I have forgotten to give an account of the charming time we had at the concert last Wed. night. After considerable opposition on the part of Mr. & Mrs. S—— which almost decided *me* not to go, they gave a reluctant consent. Mr. Phillips did not make the least objection from the first. Mr. Engelbrecht was enthusiastic, declaring if it rained he would send hacks for us, & if any girl was too poor he would send her a ticket. All of us did go except four. Even some of the sick recovered. We had seats together on the right hand in the town hall, & took them our hearts beating high with expectation. Those who were to afford us so much pleasure were "Mlle. Teresa Parodi, M. Maurice & Mde Amelia Patti Strakosch & Leonardi the Baritone." First Strakosch appeared who plays beautifully then Mde. who looked perfectly horrid in a blue gauze black hair pompadore dressed with red flowers much colour supposed not to be her own! Next the great Parodi presented herself in pink gauze decidedly "bas" a vast amount of jewelry & she remarkably *un*pretty. But she has a splendid voice. Afterwards I liked Patti almost as well & thought her much better looking. The way she trilled Mavourneen was exquisite. Strakosch plays splendidly, when will I pretend to equal him!

After all was over the audience screamed, they stamped, they knocked for the "Marsaillaise". No one appeared, "The Marsaillaise" the M——" no one—still louder!! Strakosch came up. "Ladies gentlemen, Mlle. regrets exceedingly she will ruin her voice if she sings more, it has been strained to the utmost. She. She." with a desperate effort putting his hand to his throat, "In short she *can't*." We left. Mr. Coleman sat near us wild with excitement. Celie de Rinzie looked *lovely*. As we entered the Institute door again we all simultaneously exclaimed "we've come to jail again."

Night.

I am in Lizzie Mullikin's room, she has fallen asleep her roommates and mine are all at church. The only sounds I hear are the low tones of the worshipper & her idoll alais Bec. & Sue. I must take time to tell of our day with Bec. Chapman. She is such a dear little thing. It was strange to be in a private family once more. The dinner was delightful; such turkey, fish, peas, ice cream, marmelade, pound cake, jelly, pineapples, & ginger etc. for hungry school girls. Old Mr. & Mrs. Kenney, Miss Eliza & John Chess were the other inmates. Celie de R—— & of the Institutes, *we five* Ellen Pollard, Mary Pendleton, & Mallie Price composed the guests. After dinner John Marshall, Major Kenney, Roderick Dew, & Charlie Picket came in. The idea of Mr. S——'s lambs being in such close contact with the wolves was terrific. Roderick Dew was the nicest of them all I think.

20th.

Each rolling week brings us nearer *home.* But Mr. W—— told us we ought not to wish our life two months shorter. Well I don't, but I can't help wanting the time to come to go home.

We heard a beautiful sermon from Mr. Cumming beautiful in language, in illustration in comparison, but it seemed to me it was all flowers all gestures, without much solidity. We also heard him lecture on the types of Mod. infidelity.

We are all getting our spring clothes, our bonnets are all to be trimmed with white. We want tomorrow evening to come so much so that Mr. Coleman may finish an exciting book "One Year of Wedlock." We read or hear so few stories now they make a strong impression. I feel like having something to console me this evening if I was only at West Point. O for some breeze strong enough to blow me there. What a little goose I must have been. I was telling the girls last night of my exploits with —— that delightful Spring when Annie & I reigned Queens supreme of the Superintendant's house. I think that young monsieur must "have carried on" extensively as well as some other grey coats I might mention. But I was a young lady then though one of thirteen & now—I am only an *insignificant* schoolgirl!

It seems to me I say very little of my schoolmates, but there is not much of any interest to say. Some are pretty, some are sweet, some are je ne sais quoi. My partner for breakfast & dinner is Mary Pendleton. Lizzie W—— is my sweet little beau for tea. There will be great haste when the gong sounds tonight for we have cakes! We are very much interested & absorbed in our studies, I think it is delightful to study. As for writing my thoughts, I am generally in a hurry, or there is talking, indeed we haven't much time for thinking.

May 4th.

I have been sick with chills. All the books in the Institute were collected for me to read, & I read one or two dozen. It was refreshing after studying for so long.

26th.

I can think of nothing, talk of nothing, hope for nothing now but going home. O how I long to be there to be with them *once* more. What a moment of joy when we spring on the dear old steps. There are sixteen cases of measles in the house. Mrs. Sheffey has just been in & says she is almost dead her feet are so sore she can scarcely touch the ground. She is indefatigable trying to alleviate the sufferings of the sick. A week ago, Mr. Wheat took many of us to the Blind Asylum, I should like to write of our visit & sweet little Kitty & Betty. Sat. we spent a pleasent homelike day at Cousin Anne Berkeley's. Mrs. S. came for us at nine, we had a charming walk home, & stood on the steps gazing at the beautiful stars for some time.

Cousin John Goldsborough came to see us last Thursday night. It was delightful to see any one from home. Annie was ——— so I ran down alone & had an animated time. On the steps *Drusy*! asked me in an anxious manner if Mr. *Goldbug* was my cousin. I informed her it was none of her business that cousin or no I was going to see him. Sister is enjoying herself on the Eastern Shore. We are going to be examined on Rhetoric. I dread it for I don't believe I know two questions *properly* in the book. I wrote to Papa yesterday just think I forgot to send my love to Lieuts. Dick & Jones etc. We are all preparing for the Exhibition, Annie, Ada, & I are to play.

Arlington, August 30th.

Well! I think I am the last person to keep a journal. Three months have passed or rather flown since I have written a line—You see I am at my long thought of home, have passed two charming months. We left S—— the 2nd of July. Our "Exhibition" took place the night of the 1st. The room was ornamented with Evergreens—the girls dressed in white muslin—the senior class in white sashes, middles blue, juniors pink. I had a pleasent time it was not nearly so "fearful" as I had expected. I actually smiled—even laughed while performing my terrible Witches' dance. It seemed so preposterous *my* playing at an Exhibition! Medals & diplomas were given. I received two of the former one for Scholarship & Deportment, the other Composition. I subjoin the "programme of the Exhibition at the V.F.I. Tuesday July 1st 1856."

Part 1st
Overture "Barbier de Seville" Duet, Miss Stith, Mr. Saur.
"Kathleen Mavourneen" Song Miss Johnston
Composition "Association" Miss Pollard
"Valse Sentimentale" Miss C. Stalnaker
Com. "Purposes of life" Miss Pendleton
"There's a sigh in the heart" Misses Stratton, Moncure, Argyle
"Witches' dance" Paganini Miss A. Lee
Com. "Passing away" Miss McChesney

Part 2nd
Duet from "Norma" Misses Maupin & Morgan
"Country girls" Song. Misses Stratton, Argyle, Moncure
"Musical Rockets" Miss A. Stuart
"Star Spangled banner" vocal Misses Stratton Croxton
Var. brillante "La Violette" Miss Lee
Del. Conte Grand duetto Misses Stratton, Argyle

Valedictory Miss C. Morgan
Response Miss N. R. Smith
Grand Fan. Dram. Lucia de Lammermoor, M. Argyle.

Part 3rd
Distribution of Honours
Te Deum
Benediction   R. H. Phillips

When all was over we immediately were sent upstairs but not to sleep until towards morning.

Oct. 20th, Staunton.
[Agnes' second year at Virginia Female Institute]

I am alone—I am sick I am at Staunton what more do I want to make me unhappy, even the intelligence of the death of my poor little cat, "Tomtit" might add another drop to my cup of sorrow— but I will not complain my precious papa, who is so far away, told me not to. But the "chicken-pox" is tormenting. Here I have been for four or five days with the prospect of as many more. My schoolmates have been very kind I like them better this year. I feel so much more confident in myself so much more independent! I have just received a doleful little letter from Preciosa giving the particulars of Tomtit's decease, I am so sorry he is dead he was such a pet of mine.

We have many new girls—fully eighty boarders. Two new governesses. Talbot has gone.

Feb. 8th.

I have not written in my journal for a long long time so I now must glance at myself & family this Sunday night. Grandpa, Mamma

School report of Agnes Lee, found pasted in the journal scrapbook, saved, no doubt, because it was a perfect report! Courtesy of Mrs. W. Hunter deButts.

Sister & Milly are at home. I cannot say dear Mamma's rheumatism is any better. My precious Papa is far away on the plains of Texas. Custis I know not where, either in Savannah or on Amelia Island. Rooney has returned to Arlington for his six weeks vacation. Rob. at school at Mr. Lippitt's. We at the V.F.I. Six of us now in our old room. Mary Carter returned with Annette. We five are grave & reverend seniors! S—— is the same little monotonous place, —I believe I will turn into a log. But I like our studies very much. Mr. Phillips is —— but I like & admire him for so many things I can't take time to define that liking. But he is the most refined, most *gentlemanly* person I know in S—— & is very kind to me. Mr. Wheat is the very same & Mr. & Mrs. Sheffey are old acquaintances. Miss Hooker, a northern lady is now our governess, sweet Miss Kate has a little school of her own. Mlle. Leonie Durand is rather pretty, decidly frenchy, restless, talkative— teaches french & drawing. We spent our Christmas here very pleasently. Had four invitations, three of which we accepted, just think of it! Christmas day we spent at Mr. Phillip's. Annette & I went to a little party at Miss Eddie Bell's, had a very funny time. One charming evening we passed with "Cousin Kate"—another most charmingly at an entertainment given by Misses Stevenson & Mitchell No 2, second floor. Nell & Lizzie Wilmer made *admirable* waiters. Now we have returned to our studies to study hard I hope.

Arlington Once More

The 16-year-old graduate of the Virginia Female Institute returned to Arlington in the summer of 1857. The last pages of her journal signal the end of childhood and the entrance into the joys and sorrows of maturity. The passage recording her decision to be confirmed in the Episcopal Church at Easter reveals her innate piety expressed in the language of her time. But her outpouring of sorrow at the death of her grandfather Custis in October says much more about her deeply affectionate nature. The tenderness of her love and caring for her last grandparent is particularly striking today.

Shadows of the sorrow to come were already falling across her young life. "The seven" Lee children who had been so happy together were already scattered, and illness increasingly darkened the lives of those left at home. Only two years remained to them at Arlington; in 1861 the outbreak of the Civil War would close it to them for all time.

The first entry in the journal is full of a child's excitement at Christmas. The last, written on 3 January 1858, also mentions the holiday, but briefly: ". . . we were very quiet and sad." Agnes' joy in life is still evident, but it is clear that she is learning the first lesson of adulthood, that our days are woven of both brightness and darkness. Her last sentence tells us that 1857 was "one of the happiest and the saddest I have ever numbered."

*Sketch of Arlington made by Markie Williams for her brother Orton, 1843.
Courtesy of the Arlington House Collection.*

[?] August, 1856

Dr. Stuart was our kind escort, Rooney met us in A—— & "the five cousins" came home with us where we found Rosalie Stuart & Mildred Carter. Henry Robinson came over that evening & Wassie Stuart spent the next day with us.

We found my darling Mamma sick upstairs with *rheumatism!*[99] She is better now, Mary, Rooney, Rob, & herself spent three weeks

99. Rheumatism—Mrs. Lee had a bad hip which eventually caused her to become an invalid. This would be known today as rheumatoid arthritis.

at the Va. Springs this summer & they were beneficial. During their absence Grandpa, Annie & I paid Aunt Maria a visit at Ravensworth. Chudie & Johnie[100] were there & we enjoyed ourselves highly. We have seen a good deal of Fitzhugh he is now a bvt. 2nd Lt. in *"Our"* regiment. The first time he came over with *Mr. Carroll.* I had a good deal to say to the ex-quisite! We have had a great deal of company. Roon has returned to Cambridge.

Sept. 14th.

This is Sunday night and Oh!—I am weary of being wicked! but when will I be better. Never, never I fear. Today I had hoped I might pass this *one* day as I ought, but alas I know I have been worse than ever. How I wish I could *ever* be pure & holy. I long for some one to lead me in the right way but my pride—or I fear my indifference prevents me from asking. I have too the bible, my *sense* but still I draw back from following. I know I break God's commandments every minute, *all* my thoughts are wicked & vain, but this knowledge leaves me there. Time rolls into eternity, & here I stand without being saved, without asking aid.

Aug. 16th Arlington. [1857]

I have been reading over a burst of sorrow at my own wickedness, written last summer. As I feared, that passed away—but thanks adoring thanks I trust I will ever render to my Father in Heaven that He did not leave me to sin & death as I richly deserved. In His great mercy His spirit again came to me. & in His love He called me to himself. It was at Staunton. Bishop Johns was to administer the rite of Confirmation Easter. During the Spring we had been studying McIlvaine's Ev. of Christianity. I was deeply impressed it,

100. Johnie—one of Fitzhugh Lee's brothers.

it made me *realize* what it was I believed; the evidences were clear & sufficient that there was a God. O the importance of preparing for that after life when we would dwell with Him, or be vanished from His presence forever!

One Sunday evening, I remember it well, for some forgotten cause I did not go to church. Nannie G—— & I sat in Mrs. Sheffey's room before a bright fire talking. I felt so restless so dissatisfied with myself I could not help being contradictory & disagreable. Presently I jumped up, went to my own room with the consciousness of having distressed a friend & having made myself absurd. The sound of weeping met my ear—I could not but know the cause—sorrow for sin. Did this make me feel any better, I knowing I was just as sinful & could not even weep for it? I remember how unhappy I was for days. The tempter insisted my feelings would not last, I would soon forget so I must tell *no one.* I must not show anything was the matter with me. Oh! I did endure them. God seemed only just & terrible. His glorious presence was always there, but always hidden behind an angry black cloud that ever over *me.* It seemed ever just ready to burst upon me—& far beyond I faintly felt was the light of the glorious King in his beauty *ever forever* unattainable. My sins seemed arrayed before me in all their hideousness, I was so low, so insignificant could I *dare* to imagine God would interest Himself in *me.* O do not make me speak of those days of doubt of dispair. I tried to conceal what I felt—my sorrow, my *fear,* was even so mad as try not to think of it all. I well remember a sweet friend gently holding fast my arm saying "Agnes what is the matter, you are *so* strange, tell me?" O I *longed* to tell her all, but she was not a christian, she would be amused at any one so bad as I was trying to have God's love, so I left my heart almost breaking to answer "Nothing"! At last the Saviour's, *my* Saviour's words seemed sent to suit my feelings, "He that cometh to me I will in *nowise* cast out." I clung to that. Gradually hope did come, I wrote to dear Mamma, a friend wrote

& talked to me, O after many harassing doubts & wicked want of faith I dared to be confirmed & to take the communion afterwards. Annie, Mary, Ada & Annette took the same step. Mr. Latane, our teachers were very kind. Bishop Johns spoke so beautifully to us. Those bright Easter days come back so vividly. They were happy & *blessed* too.

Sunday eve. Oct. 11th 1857.

How can I *write* it when I cannot—*cannot* (let me not say *will* not believe it. But oh! that cold white form—so *very* cold—in *death*, will come before me and make me believe *all all* my bereavement. I have no grandparent. My precious Grandpa! O come to me—come to your suffering grandchild. He cannot. My Saviour, may I believe it? He has gone where he would not wish to return. But I am left without a Grandpa. I must not murmur so but let me write *something*, just to try to relieve my bursting heart. I sometimes think I *can't* stand it. Who will supply his place to me? O no one, *no one*! Grandpa May I meet you in Heaven above? O Jesus will you not—you who are so kind, so pitying to your poor children, you who were willing to *die* for me, will you not grant that we may meet in that other world? We knew death had to come. I trust I am grateful that he was given to us for so long. But each year I prized him more, I have sometimes thought what inducement would make me willingly give up, but I still clung to him— besides I seemed so young to think of death. But *now*, What am I— What are we all without a Grandpa? What is Arlington without its master? None can ever fill *his* place. So kind he was, so indulgent, loving us so fondly, humouring our childish caprices, grateful for our little kindnesses. And now there is left to us that still vault like chamber *so* still, *so* cold—and he extended *stiller—colder*. I know I am incoherent, but such wild thoughts rush o'er my soul. I strive in vain to give vent to my burning bursting brain. I write words which don't seem to mean what I feel. Grandpa, I don't mean to murmur, but indeed it is so hard. Yesterday? Ages rather. the blank the waste is so long so broad in my young life—I cannot cover it.

Tuesday night 13th.

This is the day of *his* funeral. He whom I so dearly love is hidden from my sight; though I may have a long life I will never have again a Grandpapa. O does not this teach me not to *love life,* as I have been doing? O may the treasures of those who remain of us be laid up in Heaven. God, in your mercy grant that my father, my mother, my sisters & brothers may be spared to me, & teach me to prize this rich blessing *now*. I think he has been failing ever since my return from Berkely.[101] After spending three happy weeks at home after leaving S—— a graduate, I went with Rooney to join Mamma & Annie at B——. Custis was with us too on a short leave before going to California.[102] Mary Childe was with Mamma, so we had a charming family party. The baths were delightful but after two weeks, I came home to be with *Grandpa* & Cousin Markie, Sister having just left for the W.S.[103] How thankful I am I did return & how grateful *he* was. I then, more than ever before, ministered to his wants, sought his comforts, & prized his companionship. O how much & how undeservedly he thanked me. Mamma & Annie came home the 1st Sept., Mary not long after. Rooney had entered the Army & was at Governor's Island. He seemed to be aware of his approaching end. We saw it, but oh in

101. Berkely—Berkeley Springs, Virginia, a spa visited to help Mrs. Lee's rheumatism.

102. California—Custis had been assigned to work on Fort Point, on the San Francisco Bay.

103. W.S.—probably White Sulphur Springs, now West Virginia, another spa. The Lees went here often after the war.

my heart I could not realize it! Others told us he would be well &
strong when cold weather came & I tried to say it & *believe* it too.
But often he spoke as if his death was near at hand & would ask
God to bless him.

On the 3rd he was so ill, the Dr's & our persuasions induced him
(which in all his sicknesses he would hardly ever do) to go to bed.
I knew he would be much more comfortable, but I remember
well, my whole form trembled & my heart beat with a vague
terror, I would have given anything to have held him back as he
passed that door. Mamma, Annie & I nursed him through his short
sickness. O that is another mercy I trust I feel truly thankful for,
God's permitting me to be at home *then*, to have been absent only
three weeks during the summer—alas! three weeks too many. I
nursed him as well as I knew how, if tender love & heartfelt
prayers could aught effect I humbly trust mine have. And my
precious Grandpa was always thanking us saying "he a poor old
man was giving so much trouble." I thought it no trouble then,
only a great privilege how doubley trebly so now. Wednesday Dr.
Riley gravely said "it is no use to conceal it—at any rate from the
family he is in great peril *he can not live.* It is a pure case of
congestion of the lungs, were he young the recuperative powers of
nature might throw it off, but as he has just observed to me there
is no particular pain or disease but a general decay of the constitution, he seems perfectly conscious of it." This was our knell. And
he was conscious, said his temporal affairs were arranged, when
Sister, Cousin Markie, & Mildred arrived he knew them. O it
would be impossible to tell how patient he was how very submissive—winning nay commanding our love more than ever, so
grateful for the slightest attention—thanking me *blessing* me so
sweetly. It was shortly after midnight—Sat. morning Oct. 10th. We
were all summoned to take leave of him at the request while he
knew us. Solemn & holy was that scene, I felt the presence of
death. He remembered Papa & Custis, said Mamma must do the

best about Rooney's marriage, talked with us a short time & then asked earnestly for Mr. Dana. When he came he talked to him of the change so soon to take place, regretted very much he had never taken the holy communion, told Mr. Dana he knew the only way to be saved was through the blood of Jesus Christ, & then he joined his hands "God be merciful to me—this is all I can do" & the hands fell. I knew this was to come I had talked of it, I *thought* I was resigned! His painful breathing grated still more harshly; we were all gathered in that room, awaiting the speedy flight of the soul. "God have mercy on me in my last moments" he feebly breathed. He had said before, "I am so thankful I leave a pious family & lay me beside my blessed wife", & other words we could not hear. In the morning he became unconscious. I'd hear him murmur "I cannot see" & when the Doctor poured a little brandy in his mouth "Don't" he said, "you know I never liked spirit." About twelve A.M. the gurgling sound suddenly ceased—quietly, peacefully as an enfant he passed to his rest, we fondly prayerfully trust to that rest the Lord has prepared for those to whom he shows mercy. O my heart was breaking then—I knelt at his side, I pressed his hands pressed my burning face to them but the rushing blood the scalding tears were vain to bring heat life back— They laid him down so cold so stiff all *all* covering—face all so cold so white. beautiful flowers, dark autumn leaves made him whiter—colder. It is there! ever in my memory. Don't tell me that sixteen can't feel grief—anguish. If my lips were young the cup tasted bitter O so bitter, they trembled on the rim, they drank slowly, hesitatingly, though I knew "My Father" gave it. He is my last! Never can I do away with the past. Arlington my Grandpa & My Grandma they are the distinct spots in my child's life. Outwardly I may grow cheerful, talkative cheerful trifling—but for a long time when I write or think my thoughts must turn to them so sadly so fondly.

Rooney came before the funeral. They buried him beside his

"blessed wife". Every one was very kind, many, crowds—of the so called "great", the obscure, soldiers, servants, all drew near to pay this last tribute to one who in life had been so kind. The morning was very bright but O it was a sad sad day.

Dec. 13th.

Almost Christmas, but oh! how differently I hail its approach now from what I did in my childish days. No anticipated pleasure— what *no* pleasure? can I not welcome it as the birthday of my Saviour? The day that years ago he commenced his life or sorrow for *me*. Give me faith & love Father I need it so much.

I go to Balt. after Christmas to stay with Mary Childe[104] & take lessons in various branches. It will be very pleasent on many accounts, M—— is so kind & gay & to see dear Aunt Anne will be a great inducement, but dear dear Arlington my home of joy & sadness I cannot bear to leave it—& Papa & Mamma—& all of them I shall miss them & long for them very much.

Jan. 3rd 1858.

I have commenced to live another year—& with a sad sad heart. Yet I trust & know this is a season intended for my discipline, & though I have not a light heart—may it be submissive nay cheerful. I am going to make a few resolutions for '58, 1st, to rise earlier, 2nd, to strive to be *gentle*. 3rd, to take good care of my "good intentions." 4th, to pay greater attention to morning & evening prayer & to reading my bible. To avoid many small failings which are as well remembered & above all to be a better Christian, not in my own strength but imploring aid from my Saviour. O May I love Jesus more, my heart is so hard & cold. But two of the

104. Mary Childe—Mary Custis (Childe) Hoffman (d. 1867).

Later pictures of Arlington, found in the notebook containing the Journal and Recollections.
Courtesy of Mrs. W. Hunter deButts.

"seven" were absent this Christmas, Custis & Rooney. But we were very quiet & sad. Cares & perplexities weigh upon us all & I sometimes feel, I can't be happy again as I once was. Alas! I am no longer a free thoughtless child, at sixteen I am but too truely commencing the *battle of life* '57 has past forever. O what joys it has borne from *me*. I look back; first upon those happy school days, those cold months, when careless girls to-gether we gave our whole time to our studies, enjoying the pleasure of gaining knowledge, while our *hard* lessons, our momentary annoyances were the subject of many a laugh & threat of vengeance. Then Annie's sickness & leaving—my frantic longings for home, quite solaced by our charming ride that beautiful morning, in Mr. Phillip's carriage, when Annie went to the cars, & then so busy I could hardly miss her. Those two happy months, our last in S——. A mingling of hard study (*such* large doses of "Butler"), expectation, trepidation, speculation, animation & ambition, the luxury of 'plenty to do & to have to do it.' So many places to visit so much to see. Our beautiful walks, & that day of days to be remembered for pleasure, our trip to Weyer's cave. Our examinations, our visiting, the visit of our University cousins & lastly the Exhibition. Afterwards our merry ride home young *graduates*.[105] It all seems a dream of fairyland now. And have I forgotten the period of my conversion amid all this pleasure, that solemn Easter time when we five cousins came forward with others to take their vows of love & duty to God. What a warm young heart I had then, my prayers came from an earnest soul "Lord teach me to pray."

Those days have all gone by too, as well as those happy ones during the summer. My return from Berkely to be with my precious Grandpa. And then O then sorrow truely came, he we so loved went from us. But even then I did not feel as I do now.

57 has indeed been a year of incident, of *thought* in my short life. One of the happiest & the saddest I have ever numbered.

105. Graduate—A graduate from the V.F.I. had roughly the equivalent education of two years of college.

The Cadet Graduating Song and the poem that follow were taken from a "commonplace book" kept by the Lee sisters. These two are copied in Agnes' hand, but the scrapbook includes a variety of subjects and pieces that struck the differing fancies of the younger girls.

A CADET GRADUATING SONG

This world we may find a rough hard world,
   As we travel its mazes through—
But with right stout hearts, we'll play our parts,
    When we change the grey for the blue.
     Hurrah! Hurrah! for the merry bright month of June,
       That opens a life so new,
    When we doff the cadet and don the brevet,
      And change the grey for the blue.

To the struggles of youth to the music of war,
   To our sports and our follies adieu,
We are now for the strife, in the battle of life,
    When we change the grey for the blue.
                Hurrah! etc.

Though broken the tie that has bound us awhile,
   Fate ne'er shall dissever the few,
Of the true hearted band who linked hand in hand
    Change together the grey for the blue,
                Hurrah! etc.

As the grey of the morning is warmed by the sun,
   To the azure of noon's bright hue,
So, the morn of our time ripens fast to its prime,
    When we change the grey for the blue.
                Hurrah! etc.

The members of the "Mind your own business society" propose for consideration the following

QUERIES

"If a person feels a person treading on his toes
Need a person ask a person how a person knows?"
"Is it anybody's business if a gentleman should choose
To wait upon a lady if the lady don't refuse?"
Or to speak a little plainer, that the meaning all may know
Is it anybody's business if a lady has a beau?"

Is it anybody's business
When the gentleman does call
Or when he leaves the lady
Or if he leaves at all?
Or is it necessary
That the curtain should be drawn
To save from further trouble
The outside lookers on?

Is it anybody's business
But the lady's, if her beau
Rides out with other ladies
And does not let her know?
Is it anybody's business
But the gentleman's if she
Should accept another escort
Where he does not chance to be?
The substance of our query
Simply stated would be this
"Is it anybody's business
What another's business is?"
If it is or if it isn't
We would really like to know
For we're certain if it isn't
There are *some* who make it so.

Berkely Springs Aug. 4th/57

Part Two
Recollections by Mildred Lee

A little over three years after the last entry in Agnes's journal, the guns opened fire on Fort Sumter and the Civil War began on 12 April 1861. Few things bring home the reality of this war as does the knowledge that the young cadets Agnes described would be killing each other in battle after battle as the world she knew came to an end.

The life of the Lee family, along with so many others, was drastically changed. In May 1861 Mrs. Lee left Arlington forever and she and her four daughters wandered homeless, visiting relatives and friends until settling in Richmond early in 1864. Lee and his sons saw active duty in the Confederate Army but all survived the war. Annie died while visiting friends in North Carolina; Rooney was wounded and captured, and while he was in prison, his wife Charlotte and their two small children died; Orton Williams, on a mission behind the Union lines, was caught and hanged as a spy.

Five months after Appomattox General Lee accepted the presidency of Washington College in Lexington, Virginia, and late in 1865 he once more had a home for his wife and daughters. The three Lee sons went to work—Custis taught at the nearby Virginia

The president's house at Washington College in Lexington, Virginia, the Lees' last home. A house on the campus was provided for them when they first arrived. The house in this picture was built under the direction of President Lee, and he and his wife and daughters moved into it in 1869. Courtesy of the Michael Miley Collection, Washington and Lee University.

Military Institute, and Rooney and Rob farmed the lands left them by their grandfather Custis in New Kent and King William Counties, respectively.

In the spring of 1870 the Trustees of Washington College, realizing that Lee's health was precarious and that he was worrying about what would happen to his wife in the event of his death, worked out a proposal to convey the president's house to Mrs. Lee for her lifetime and to provide her with an income. When told of this, General Lee expressed his appreciation but refused the offer. For probably the first time since his taking office as president, the Trustees did not agree with a decision of General Lee's and without any argument quietly left this resolution on the books. As it happened, their kind thought and generosity were hardly needed. Lee died in October 1870 and Custis Lee was made president of the college, then renamed Washington and Lee. Agnes and Mrs. Lee

Interior of president's house when the Lees lived there.
Courtesy of Washington and Lee University.

both died in the autumn of 1872, but Custis' other sisters were still able to call Lexington their home, and it was there many years later that Mildred wrote her recollections—the Garden at Arlington and the Death of Agnes.

None of the Lee family ever lived at Arlington after the Civil War. General Lee had hoped for a time to regain possession for his wife, but his efforts were not successful. After the death of both his parents, Custis Lee, who had inherited Arlington from his grandfather Custis, took legal action to obtain it. In 1882 the case was decided in his favor by the Supreme Court of the United States, which ruled that Arlington had been taken illegally. However, by that time thou-

Robert E. Lee, President of Washington College.
Courtesy of the Virginia Historical Society.

Mrs. Robert E. Lee at Lexington.
Courtesy of Mrs. W. Hunter deButts.

sands of U.S. soldiers had been buried on the grounds and Custis Lee accepted the government's offer of $150,000 for the property in lieu of possession.

In 1887 Custis left Washington and Lee and lived until his death in 1913 at Ravensworth, Fairfax County, which belonged to his brother Rooney (Fitzhugh), who died in 1891. The surviving daughters of General Lee, Mary and Mildred, traveled or visited their brothers and friends until Mildred's death in 1904, after which Mary took an apartment in Washington, D.C., where she died in 1918.

Feb 5th. 1884

11 years since Agnes died!

I wish to recall her last words, knowing how treacherous memory is. She had been ill for weeks, but I never realized it—absorbed in housekeeping, company, everything but the comfort of the dear frail form that was so soon to leave us. God knows my remorse now, when I remember my carelessness! About the 1st. of Oct I was roused to a sense of her danger—& moved her from our old room to a brighter sunnier one. She had to lean on me as we crossed the passage, & entered her death chamber, not to leave it until she was carried out in her coffin by her three brothers. Oh, those golden Oct days! The delicious sunshine thro the open windows, the roses, whose days were also numbered! I used to place them so her tired eyes could drink in their beauty. The sound of the stone-masons, cutting away at the church opposite—went on through those weary days. She said she liked to hear it—"how strong *they* must be"! Looking down at her own white hands. I forget what day Jinnie Ritchie came—she rode over from the Baths to inquire—and staid until it was over. A ministering angel she was, sitting up *every* night—so strong & cheerful & helpful.

The 12th Oct came—the day my Father died. She was very ill.

I rode out in the afternoon with poor Mr. Davidson to get some air, she telling me to go, & brought back branches of crimson leaves, with which I decorated his picture on the mantlepiece. She looked, but said nothing. But afterwards (the next day 13th) she spoke of it gratefully, & said "don't think I am not appreciative of all this kindness & nursing, because I am silent, but if you knew how much I suffered"!

On the morning of the 14th I was combing her soft brown hair— her eyes had an unearthly brilliancy—& occasionally looking heavenward. The Doctor (Graham) was sent for, & told us she had but a short time to live!

In the afternoon my poor suffering mother was brought up in her chair, & sat close to her bedside holding her hand, the tears streaming down her face, but Agnes was hardly concious—the stupor of death was gathering fast. Later about dusk her mind cleared, & turning to the Doctor said to my surprise, "Doctor must I prepare to live or die"? "To do both Miss Agnes." He went out, & we were left alone. She must have seen my tearful eyes, & said, "it is just as well. I never cared to live long. I am weary of life." "How strange I should die between my Father & Annie. He died on the 12th Annie on the 20th"! "You must thank Dr. Graham & Dr. Barton for their kindness—they did what they could." "Mildred you must look after my God-children—give my watch to Katherine, & my lace shawl & little work-box to Sally Poor & her little daughter. Little Mildred can have my old clothes—you Mildred must look over my letters & papers. I suppose those that are of no use had better be destroyed. "Perhaps Cousin Markie had better have my *Bible*—you know *Orton* gave it to me"! Then the stupor came on again, & the shadows gathered. I have written exactly what I can remember, but fear I may have lost some precious words. Night drew on—the stars shone & glittered—the fire blazed on the hearth. We were all collected in that still room, looking wistfully at the slight form on the bed, & listening to her breathing. Dear Jinnie Ritchie was putting hot irons to her feet—Cousin Markie doing all she knew how. I was stretched upon the floor, my head splitting with a raging headache. We had induced Mama to go to bed. The Doctor was lying down in Custis' room, & Custis was resting in a little back room. I was doing something for Agnes after awhile, when she opened her eyes, & asked in a ringing tone, that will sound forever in my ears—"Am I dying"? I said "Oh Agnes I am afraid you are—you are not afraid to die"? "No," & she said something about "My Saviour," & "going to my Father," (meaning Papa) & "lay me by my Father." We all stood breathless around her bed. I managed to repeat the Lords Prayer, & she joined in at "*Forgive* us our trespasses," murmuring "ah that's the part"! Then Jinnie Ritchie said, "would you like me to say "Rock of Ages"? She assented, & listened while those solemn words were repeated in a firm voice. "Where is Custis"? I ran for him. He sat on the bed by her side, & she said in a half caressing way, "you know I have always loved you—you must not forget me when I am gone." He stroked her hand, saying "Aggie none of us will do that." All of us were so choked with sobs we could not speak. She turned to me. "Mildred take care of the Conors (a poor family) for my sake." "Mildred, you will forgive my being exacting at times—you know I was always *contrary*"! I forget now what else she said. I remember saying "you are going to Papa, & Annie & GrandMa", & her again murmuring "by my Father." "Annie"—That was all—her breathing grew shorter—one gasp—& all was over for ever!

Day was just about dawning in the East, when her pure, her heroic spirit took its flight—ah *whither*, who can tell! I rushed down stairs to tell Mama. Shall I ever forget that scene— She was standing undressed in the chilly frosty morning air, my poor suffering, patient Mother, & when I told her Agnes was dead, cried "my poor child, that I should have outlived her. Oh that I could have seen her again"! Mama never rallied from this blow, & died on the 5th Nov. less than a month after.

Agnes Lee at Lexington.
Courtesy of Mrs. W. Hunter deButts.

I laid two roses on Agnes' dead heart, gathered from the bush Papa planted—and on the 17th Oct she was laid beside her Father in the Chapel, where soon after my precious Mother was also taken—& buried close to the side of her beloved husband.

Agnes was between 32 & 33—just ten years older than *Annie* when she died.

Mildred Lee

Lexington. July 20th 1890

Today in church, a stranger sang "Jesus Saviour of My Soul" in a rich sweet voice—instantly my thoughts flew to the old garden at Arlington—to a wooden bench, almost hidden by a drooping branch of seringa, my favorite hiding place in those days of long ago. There I used to sing that hymn & pray to be good, like the various saintly characters in Grand Ma's religious Biographies, and my heart did glow with a certain fervour, but whether it was hatred of sin, or delight in the sweet starry blossoms, I cannot well tell!

I wish I could paint that dear old garden! In all parts of the world I have seen others, adorned & beautified by Kings & Princes, but none ever seemed so fair to me, as this Kingdom of my childhood.

A large arbour stood in the centre, covered with heavy masses of yellow Jasamine, & every morning we children found the ground beneath carpeted with the golden blossoms, which we gathered & made into necklaces, or long strings to be put in the linen. As for the roses, I can go in spirit to each one, & tell you its name, & *remember* its vanished perfume! These damask and hundred-leaf roses are sweetest of all, & were used in making rose-water which "Nurse" & "Mammy" used to make & keep in tall bottles in the storeroom. Annie loved the dark red roses, & the deep yellow, tipped with crimson—they looked well in her glossy

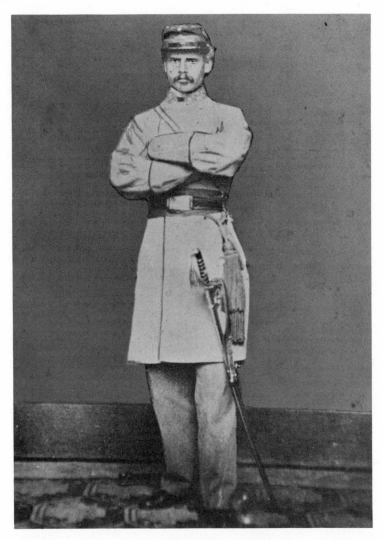

William Orton Williams, Agnes Lee's unsuccessful suitor. Williams lost his life for the Confederacy.
Courtesy of Mrs. W. Hunter deButts.

black hair. Papa was very fond of gathering roses before breakfast, & putting them at the plate of each lady. I can see now the delicate buds of the Safronia on the old blue china! He would give *me* a very small bud, & fuller blooms to the older ladies. I have never seen lilies of the valley grown in such beauty & profusion; great fields of them under every evergreen & shady place, planted there by my Grand Mother, who dearly loved them.

Big snow ball bushes, purple & white lilacs, behind which we played Hide & Seek! Mock Orange, maiden's bower, honney suckle, where the humming bird loved to linger—crocuses peeping thro the snow—jonquils, hyacinths in the early spring—cowslips & violets in all the borders—all come back to me, with a message from the Dead! I remember one evening Annie & Agnes making me a wreath of the single red roses that grew under the apricot tree. I wore it with great pride on my sunny brown curls. They are now wearing in Heaven perhaps the mystical crowns of gold, promised to those who endure!

My mother spent hours here, digging, weeding, & directing "Old George," little George, Uncle Ephriam, Billy, & swarms of small ethiopians. I can see her now with a white sun-bonnet hanging down her back! Visitors from Washington, Alexandria, Georgetown, always ended by a stroll in the gardens; never leaving without armfuls of flowers.

My eldest sister Mary walked here in the gloaming with her young Army admirers—Cousin Markie with sentimental students of divinity!

The grove was a place of mystery to me! It was a part of the Park enclosed in the garden, & was the special resort of squirrels, blue bells of Scotland, & grape vines, where we used to swing. Here too there was an arbour, covered with a grape vine, with a big mossy natural stone for a seat—a capital place to crack hickory-nuts. I first read the "Dairyman's daughter", & "Corlebs in search of a wife" on this hard, damp stone! There were no English sparrows

Mildred Lee at Lexington.
Courtesy of Mrs. W. Hunter deButts.

then, & how the birds did sing—love, ever of love—that was the burden of their song in those days!

Just on the edge of the Grove, under a spreading tree, was my own little garden, a white lilac in one corner & violets forming the borders of the beds. *Harry Washington Gray*, a small darkey, was my head gardiner, & much fonder of play, than work. Here were the graves of my cats, "Thomas Chalmers," "Thomas Acquinas," etc! Ah, the burning tears I have dropped upon those graves!

It all seems a dream ... only a few months ago, I stood once more in the garden at Arlington. In place of the Jesamine arbour, was a hidious white pavilion, with the names of Lincoln, Grant, Sherman, Sheridan, etc. emblazoned in stareing black letters. Every thing was gone—the dim shady alleys, the flowering shrubs, the rose beds were replaced by stiff little beds, cut in ginger-cake patterns. . . . Everywhere, as far as my aching eyes could see, graves, graves, graves, in memory of the men who had robbed me of my beautiful home.

Farther off still, under the shadow of glorious oaks, neglected, unknown—almost hidden by the myriads of monotonous head stones, I sought the graves of my Grand Parents, who are insepa- rably associated with the old life at Arlington, & who alone, of all these countless hosts, have a right to rest in peace amid its fra- grant, flowery woods.

Mildred

Part Three
Family Letters

The Lees were an articulate family of writers. From Thomas Lee's eloquent treaty with the Indians at Lancaster in 1744, through Richard Henry Lee as southern chairman of the Secret Correspondence Committee in pre-Revolutionary days and Arthur Lee as pamphleteer and secret agent, this talent is evident. Agnes Lee's grandfather, "Light Horse Harry" Lee, wrote the definitive book on the southern department of the American Revolution, but his son Robert Edward revealed his literary gift in his correspondence. The Arlington Lees were prolific letter writers; thousands of long, detailed pages sustained the bonds of affection whenever Lees were separated. The examples included here will enhance the reader's understanding of the relationships of this extraordinary family.

The two letters from General Lee to Agnes were written during one of the most frustrating periods of his army life. The cavalry post at Camp Cooper, Texas, was in barren, rugged, largely unmapped territory 270 miles north of San Antonio. There was no lumber and therefore no buildings; Lee lived in a tent as did all the regiment. The temperature was often 112° in the shade; rattlesnakes and wolves abounded. To the north the Comanches roamed and hunted, always ready to attack a white man.

The court martial duty referred to in the letter from San Antonio was one of the most punishing for commanding officers. They were required to leave their regiments for months at a time, often riding hundreds of miles, to sit in endless inquiries. Lee described two Texas lawyers to Mrs. Lee as "accustomed to the tricks and stratagems of special pleadings, which, of no other avail, absorb time and stave off the question." But no matter where he was, or how strenuous his duties, Lee always found time to write to his family.

Agnes Lee's letters to her parents round out the picture that she gives us of herself, a lively, conscientious young girl with a sense of humor, striving to live up to the expectations of her parents, returning the love that was so abundantly given to her.

Staunton May 24th 1856.

My dearest Papa,

Annie has written to you and I can not let the letter depart without enclosing one from myself. We wrote to you some time ago, just after receiving the letter you mailed upon your departure from San Antonia, but I fear it has never reached you, it is so far & there are so many delays & I suppose it must have been lost.

I confess I have little to tell you, our only thought, our only talk, is I may say entirely about our going home! We will not be here at the farthest more than a month, scarcely that, but time *creeps* now it never seemed so long! I expect you think, dear Papa I will never learn to be *moderate,* or in fact do as I ought indeed I think so but oh! I am so tired, I want to see Ma. & Grandpa & all so much, it is so hot we can't study, so I can not help thinking and talking *only* of home. But I must not complain any more nor write you such a *doleful* letter your condition is far worse than mine, I know, my own Papa without even a prospect of coming home for a long time. I so very often think of you and want to know what you are doing, if you are happy or feel lonely, & try to picture to myself your dwelling; you must tell me all about it so I can know if you are comfortable. Is the whole regiment with you? I wish *I* was with you perhaps I would be some comfort or pleasure to you & repay in some small measure all that you have done and been to *me*! I little valued the blessing of our being all united at West Point. Now it seems to me we are so separated and so far apart. Ma. says Custis has not the slightest expectation of being home this summer. I am *so* disappointed. I had so often thought of having *him* at least with us. So we who are the most fortunate grumble the most. I am going to stop now but I have not quite recovered from chills I had the first of the week & Annie is still sick, so it makes me sad & unhappy.

We are going (at least Mary and Ada & I) to spend the evening with Cousin Ann Berkely. I like her very much she is very kind & sweet. She allways desires her love or remembrance to you when we write. We have only spent the day out once at Mr. Kinney's who has a little granddaughter from Washington staying with him, going to school here. I say *little* for she is much smaller than I am but she is fifteen or sixteen. Perhaps you know we are going to have what they call a grand "Exhibition" the night before we leave. Annie and I both have to play as well as Ada Stuart. You can't tell how frightened I am for I never can play before *anyone* much less so many persons as will be here. But I hope for the best and shall try for my parents and teachers sake to succeed.

Mr. Wheat took as many of the girls as wanted to go to the Blind, & Dumb Asylum last Saturday. It was very interesting to see those poor blind & deaf children being instructed, some were remarkably smart. One little blind girl read just as well as I do & she was only eleven. Some of the deaf & dumb had painted some beautiful flowers & the blind sung & played very sweetly. We have taken many long walks with Mr. W., in some of which I was unable to join him because I was sick, but the others I enjoyed very much though I found I was much sooner fatigued than when we used to walk on those fine old mountains at W.P. I must now stop *dearest* Papa. I hope this letter will reach you. Write very soon to us. And remember you are ever in the thoughts of your

own devoted daughter
Agnes

The girls send much love.

Excuse, dearest Papa, my writing as I was in a great hurry we have a great deal to do now preparing for our examinations.

[Endorsed by R. E. Lee]
"24 May 1856 Anne & Agnes"
"Ans[d] 4 Aug."

Camp Cooper, Texas
4 Aug 1856

I cannot send off my letters to Arlington dearest Agnes without writing to you. But what shall I tell you more than you know already. How glad I was to receive your letter (24 May) to hear from you, to talk to you. Oh, that I could see you, kiss you, squeeze you! But that cannot be Agnes & I must not indulge in wishes that cannot be gratified. That reminds me I must take you to task for some expressions in your letter. You say, "our only thought, our only talk, is entirely about our going home." How can you reconcile that with the object of your sojourn at Staunton! Unless your thoughts are sometimes devoted to your studies, I do not see the use of your being there, & if it was "so hot" (24 May) as to render it "impossible for you to study," in the mountains of Virg[a] how can you expect to exist in Texas in July & Aug. It is so hot in my tent now, that the spermaceti candles become so soft as to drop from the candlesticks. Sturine candles, have melted, & become liquid in the stand. The chair I sit in & the table I write on is *hot*, disagreeably so, to the touch, & feel as if made of metal. Do not speak of heat Agnes, for you know not what it is & I shall have to relinquish all hope of ever having you here with me. I hope notwithstanding, the great heat at Staunton & your desire to reach Arlington, you were able to prepare yourself for your "grand exhibition," & I feel assured that both you, Annie & Ada acquitted yourselves well. So tell me how you performed, how you stand in your class & all about it. I unite with you in your wishes that we were all together, & have no doubt we shall be, if it is best for us. You will still have around you, many, a great many. Your Grandfather, Mother, brothers & sisters, Custis I fear will not be able to join you. He and I must bide our time.

You say I must tell you about my dwelling. Imagine then a plain, with a high abrupt & rocky hill to the rear & north, terminated by a winding narrow river to the south, the banks of which are fringed with some magnificent pecan, elm & ash trees. On this plain, perpendicular to the crest of the hill, stand 4 parallel rows of tents, each row containing one Comp^y. A single row perpendicular to these, situated near the foot of the hill, furnish quarters for the officers. A wide avenue divides the camp in half—2 Comp^{ys} being on one side, 2 on the other. At the centre of the north end of this avenue, & a little retired behind the row of officers tents, stands the Comm^g Officers tent. That is mine. On the right is the Adjt^s & on the left the Q^r M^{rs}. At the south extremity of this avenue, advanced to the limit of the camp, stand the guard tents. Behind the Comm^g officers tent is his kitchen. Behind his kitchen is his henhouse, & behind his henhouse, is picketed his bay mare Mary. I think now you can make a picture of my domicil[e].

The interior is equally preposessing. On the right of the entrance of the tent, stands an iron camp bed. On the left a camp table & chair. At the far end a trunk. On the side near the entrance a water bucket, basin & broom, clothes hang around within easy reach of all points, & a sword & pistol very convenient. A saddle & bridle stand at the foot of the bed on a wooden horse. What more could it or ought it to contain! I am very sorry to hear you had a return of your chills this spring. I hope they will not continue through the summer & fall. You had better adopted my suggestion, & got into some decent farmhouse in the mountains, & learned to make butter & cheese, & grown strong & hearty. I fear your visits to A. will confine you in chills & fevers. Perhaps you did not get my letter. I must now bid you goodbye. Give love to everyone. Your affectionate father

R. E. Lee

Staunton, Sunday
Oct. 19th 1856

Now my precious Papa, have I not dated my letter *this* time? My conscience really reproaches me for not having written to you before, this being the 2nd letter I have received from you since I wrote, but we thought we would wait till our arrival at S—— to answer your much prized letters (Aug. 4th) & a short time after we reached here, yours of Aug. 26th were forwarded. As you say you had time to read my last I will take courage & write a long one this time. The room is perfectly quiet, every one is at church & I am its sole occupant. Perhaps you may wonder why I am not participating in the services of this holy day. Well, last Thursday morn. after returning from our walk *before* breakfast, I began to feel the most curious pains in my chest & back—indeed all over. I bore them for that day & part of the next, until a short time before dinner they grew so much worse & my head ached violently besides I was obliged to lie down. The next morning I found my face considerably covered with pistules. They increased so that in the evening the famous Dr. McGill was summoned, who, after frightenning me a little about the smallpox & saying such & such a pistule was exactly like this disease in its first stages, told me it was *chicken-*pox. Where I caught it I can't imagine, as I haven't heard of it for the longest. It is not particularly agreeable & it seems to me I am so sensitive to any breaking out I feel it more than most persons. Still if I never have greater pain than this to bear I will be far *far* more fortunate than any one beside. It does make me look so funny, if you could only see the face bending over your letter it would amuse you. Though my feelings, the smarting & burning &c extending in some degree all over me is not so laughable.

I must now tell you something about the V.F.I. (our school). They pretend to be, & indeed *are*, much stricter this year than last. We have a french & an english governess. "Mlle" teaches us drawing & I think is a much better teacher than the one last year. We are in the highest class this year under Mr. Phillips' tuition.

Our english studies for the present are Theology, French on Words, & Chemistry also Algebra. Extras, Music, Latin & drawing. I intend to practice a great deal this year. I am very fond of it now & am glad I never gave it up. Annie, Ada Stuart & myself are at the respective heads of three sections of Music, who alternate in playing at our soirées. I like Latin very much & only wish I had commenced before but Mr. P. says he thinks we can read right well this year if we try. I also feel more interested in drawing even than I did, as our teacher, *teaches* more. Annette brought Mary back with her who is in the class below us. We are all six in one room *now* but will not be so crowded when the addition to the building is completed; it will be ready to occupy by Dec. or Jan.

I am glad that this is my last year here though I don't think I will have learnt all that schools can teach me after its expiration even if I *did* say so. I am much obliged for your description of your camp & have a very good little picture of your tent on the tablet of my mind. I know exactly what to expect if I go out there, but I don't see that you have room for any addition to your family with your present accommodations. I am sure I should like to live out in Texas for a year or two so much, for besides being with you my dearest Papa, it seems to me you must always feel so *well*, in the open air, riding & walking. I want to learn to ride *well* so much. I did ride this summer at home, but little Santie is the only agreeable steed & so he is in considerable demand as much as is consistant with his age & size. Old Ann is no longer an agreeable animal because of her stumbling & uneasy gait—I suppose resulting from her increasing years. How many officers & how many men have you with you? Where is Col. Johnson? Does he ever come there, or what does he do? I am sorry your pets have disappeared. Your little mouse must have a great deal of assurance, they are generally so shy.

Tuesday night, Oct. 21. As they only mail letters here twice a week, I thought I would add a few lines tonight before committing it to the post box. When I think what a long way it has to go, it does not seem half worth the journey, but if you will recollect the suffering I was enduring while writing for ever since the appearance of the eruption it has kept up a most annoying & painful itching & burning, being in my eyes & everywhere else it was not desired, I feel sure you excuse its deficiencies. And if it will afford you any pleasure, or convey to you the least conception of how dearly I love my own Papa & how often I think of him but I fear it will not, still if it does it will not be without avail. I know you will say the best way to manifest my affection will be to do my duty & study my lessons. This I know, & *do* try but I also know not hard enough, but I have made several good resolution during my sickness which I hope earnestly I can keep. Do not be unhappy on my account dear Papa, for I don't think I ever *can* do *any*thins to make you ashamed of me though I know I am very *very* bad & just the opposite of what I *ought* to be. Perhaps as I grow older I may know how to do better. I hope I will be able to go to school tomorrow or next day & then I am going to bear in mind that I came here to *study* & so act. But I had better not tell you of what I am going to do till it is *done*? I should like very much to hear a description of a storm in camp. It must be so grand & with such a frail protection as a tent over you. I must now stop. O I wish I could kiss you Good-night. May that time come soon is the earnest wish & prayer of your

devoted daughter Agnes.

San Antonio, Texas,
11 March '57

I must thank you too, my dearest Agnes, for your welcome & nice letter of the closing day of the last year. It was very kind in you to withdraw yourself from your merry companions & devote a portion of your holy day to me. I feel very grateful for it; & though I am sorry at your disappointment in not going home, still under the circumstances I think you must feel better satisfied in doing what was right & complying with what your mother considered best for you. The time is near at hand, when you will leave school for good, & enter upon a new course of life. I hope you will find yourself prepared for it, & ready to meet all its necessities. I hardly think though, you will be willing to stop where you are, but hope you will be desirous of continuing your studies & perfecting yourself in all usefulness. I am told by the ladies here that the convent in this town affords an excellent school. Among the nuns there are capital teachers of music, french, spanish & drawing. Surely none may be deterred by its expensiveness, for the lessons seem almost gratuitous. Music is $4 a quarter, & drawing $2. There is also a separate branch of needlework, & the girls are taught to sew beautifully. Miss Nannie Wells, daughter of Dr. W—— & the two daughters of my landlady go there daily. Miss Nannie seems devoted to her studies, & I have never been to her mothers, in any of my visits to San Antonio, that I did not find her at them. Should you not have heard before this reaches you, you must now know, that the great Giles Porter Court has at length adjourned. I went from the court room to the steamer, that transported me to Ringgold Bks. & as soon after landing as I could saddle up and get provisions for the journey, I led off into the great prairie on a due north course. On the 12th mor[ning] thereafter, about three hours after sunrise, I discovered the white buildings of San Antonio, looming in the distance directly before me. After leaving the Rio Grande until I reached the Medina, about 12 miles from here, where I crossed it, I saw but a single habitation. It laid out of my path & I did not visit it, but it appeared to be what is called a Cattle Ranch in Texas. The streams are all low & I had no difficulty in crossing them. Indeed the country was so dry that I found but three running streams between here & the Rio Grande & we suffered on the prairies for water, often going all day without any, & at night sharing a muddy pool with the wild horses, the deer & the wolves. There were not however many animals on the prairies, from which they seem to be driven to the rivers by the scarcity of water. We fell in with three separate parties of Mexicans, in quest of wild horses, & I witnessed the capture of some of them. The process is too long for the limits of this letter, so I must reserve it for another time, or until we meet. One of these mustangs (the name they give the wild horses) carried off one of my mares, for which I shall not forgive him. I hope she will be happy in her freedom, though I shall miss her very much. One night I came upon the camp of Capt. Whiting, 2 Cav. He had come out in search of a party of Indians who it was said had been seen in the neighborhood of Laredo. Mr. Lowe was with him & Mr. Radziminski had been left at Fort Inge in charge of the garrison. They were about 100 miles from the Fort & marched with me the next day to the Nueces, where we parted. It is pleasant to meet in the wilderness unexpectedly with friends. I had supposed the company had been moved up on the Rio Grande to Fort Clarke, where it is ordered, & where it will go as soon as Capt. W—— returns to Fort Inge. On my arrival here I found orders from Washington sending me on another Court Martial to "Indianola, Texas" where direct if you write at once. If not, direct here as usual. I ans^d your other letters from Fort Brown, dear Agnes, which I hope you got not so much for its value but to shew you of my attention to it. I am writing as you were *against time* in your last letter. I found so many here that I am constantly occupied in replying to them. I also found Mr. and Mrs. Edwd Stockton. She was Miss Mary Cozzens of W.P. then. They also to Indianola for the present. I go in a few days. The Court is to meet on the 20th Inst. The sun is setting & the mail soon departs. Excuse haste.

Your fond father
R. E. Lee

Do not forget the cambric underskirts to our barèges.

Thursday night April 2nd.
[1857?]

Dear Mamma, Your letter has just been received and we thought it better to write at once. You made a mistake about the measure as you will see by examination. Near one end you will see "Agnes" written in pencil from that point to the other end I believe is a pretty exact measure of *my* length, the *whole* is Annie's. Annie says she does not want the *old pink* lawn but her *purple* with the body. She wants the *new* pink piece to make a *high necked* body to the dress, you know they are both *low* necked and so are not so useful at school, particularly as it will not be warm here much of the time. I want some of it also to make a cape to cover my bones, pretty generally.

We will I presume have time to make them as they will be slight work. Do not trouble yourself to get the things ready for Counsin J—— unless you can easily for I fear it will tire you too much. Indeed I think you will hardly get them from Phil. then. If you do though, we will be very glad to receive them. I believe I have told you all we wanted. Please send me a leather belt similar to those we always get in Alexandria. Mine is *completely* worn out. If you do send the things by Cousin Julia, I suppose there will be no difficulty in getting the belt, fan, thin stockings, 4 pr., gaiters, 2½ with heels please, muslin collar and linen to make another, pink lawn piece, my & Annie's *purple* lawn dresses, our exhibition dresses, *white* sashes, we are obliged to have as the kind our class have to wear, and if conveniently done please send me a tolerably small pair of lisle thread gloves. Do not forget to send the fringe for the cape and sleeves of my uniform dress and for the sleeves of Annie's, she prefers it high necked. Two brown belts to suit. Of course we would much prefer our uniform dresses and bonnets received now. I believe I asked you to make my dress tucked with narrow tucks to the waist, if you can as I do not admire the color I would like it to be as pretty as possible. Send the underskirts if made. And if there is room in the trunk, which I scarcely suppose there will be, send us some cakes or biscuits or apples &c. The girls have been so generous with their boxes I should like to have something to give them in return. Now, I hope our clothes will be done with. I would be so glad Mamma if you could go to Bath and get *perfectly well* and then come up here just before the exhibition to see your daughters graduate, go with them to Wier's cave and go home with them! It is not impracticable, is it? Above all things it would be seeing you sooner. I am going to try not to be discontented though and wait patiently till summer comes. No dearest Mamma, I will not hesitate to be confirmed. My desire grows stronger and stronger. I am sure I will feel strengthened and blessed. Much would I love to receive the holy communion also, but oh! my deep unworthiness makes me shrink from so blessed a privilege If I should dare to do so with unclean heart it would be awful. So often have I condemned others for too great inconsistency, after being received at our Lord's table; I, so much more deeply dyed in sin, fear my Savior will find me unworthy. Yet, oh! 'tis a blessed feeling to think my Savior died for me and "he that *cometh* to Him He will in no wise cast out." May I come to Him with my whole heart! I must stop, dear Mamma, excuse the awful scrawl from my great haste.

> Yours as ever,
> Agnes

Arlington Wednesday 14th
[1857?]

It is very late my precious little daughter, but I cannot let another day pass without telling you the real happiness your letter afforded me, *you* for whom I have felt so anxious, to hear that God had sent his Spirit into your heart & drawn you to himself. Remember what He says, "Those who seek me *early shall find me*" The promises of God are sure & cannot fail. Therefore *seek* Him with all your heart. Be willing to give up all for Him & He will strengthen you & give you that peace & happiness which is not to be found in this world. And then to think that your dear brother Robert has been the *means* of producing this blessed change. You must *pray* for your sister for your brothers who are out of the fold of Christ. Think what a happiness to your poor Mother to be able to present *all* her children at the *throne* of God & to be able to say 'Here I am Lord & the children Thou has given me. Pray for your Mother that she may be more faithful in her prayers & example. Commit your *all* to Christ & do not fear He will never leave you nor forsake you. He will give you strength to resist the world & to serve Him. The more faithfully you serve Him the happier you will be for "His Yoke is easy & his burden light. Have you written to Robbie to tell him this good news it will rejoice his heart. I forgot to send you any stamps, but you can buy some with the money as there are none in the House I can send you with this letter. I only sent you $2.00 which was all the change I had but if you need more before Christmas, you must let me know. Your sister has gone to Goodwood. Annie sends her love and rejoices with me in the good news & I know there is joy in the presence of the angels of God. I accept my dear child your penitence for all your faults towards me & freely *bestow* my forgiveness. Pray to God never to suffer you to fall into the like again, but to transform you into the image of his dear Son in whom was no sin, neither was guile found in his mouth.

I shall feel very anxious to hear from you again I had just given your box to your Aunt Nannie when I received your letter. I hope you will like the contents. Just hem up the worn edges of those fir cuffs & they may be of some use to you. Your Aunt Nannie will be coming down soon after you receive this you can write me a long letter by her & if you have old shoes that you do not want & that will do for Magdalena & Sarah make them into a little bundle & send them by your Aunt, you have no occasion to say what it contains, but do not rob yourself. I so long to see you & you will now be so doubly dear to me.

I cannot thank my Heavenly Father as I ought to do for all his mercy.

Good night it is 12 oclock & all are in bed.

> Your devoted & happy
> Mother M C Lee

Do not get tired of this long letter. I will be more moderate another time.

March 21st 1857.

Thank you dearest Mamma, for your letter. It did me so much good. O I hope I have found the "pearl of great price," discovered the truth the satisfying of its comforts. That I may be a child of God, a lamb in Christ's fold is my earnest prayer. I find so much comfort in prayer. Every morning I go into one of the unoccupied rooms in the new building and closing the door pray aloud for help and guidance, for my dear family, and what I feel I need. I know they are *very* weak and imperfect—but it seems to me when uttered they confine my attention better and make me feel their reality. So long have the lips framed words the heart but little felt this wicked habit clings to me and my thoughts will sometimes wander. Yes I earnestly desire to be confirmed, I feel if I make a public profession it will strengthen me. It seems to me impossible to make myself in the least pleasing in God's sight. He is so holy and I am so very wicked, I never knew, I suppose I never examined how very vile my heart was, but then I know on my own strength I never can be any better. Yet I would not give up the hopes, the peace I sometimes feel for anything. It is so delightful to feel there is some one to go to who will hear our sorrows, and grant us peace. Mr. Sheffey's and Mr. Phillips' conversations (not to me particularly but to all of the girls) are very instructive, and Mr. Latane a most faithful preacher. He preached a most beautiful sermon last Sunday upon "Seek ye the Lord, that ye may be hid in the day of his anger." One of the girls gave me an excellent letter from her pastor on the subject of not being good enough to come to Confirmation. O I feel sure I love my Savior and though I am so very wicked I will still trust in Him and however often I fail which is *always* I will strive on, not doubting "His grace is sufficient for me." It is a blessed promise "He that cometh to me I will in no wise cast out." I still have doubts and darkness but I hope and pray they will be removed.

Annie has been sick for some days with something of a bilious attack, but I think is now better.

I cannot concieve how our bill would be $469.37 for a half session. You know it would be equivalent to one for the whole session; $200. for english & board $60. for music, $60 for french latin and drawing making $320. altogether; unless they have made different charges than those I have stated and charged the extras for the whole session. Incidentals such as music, books &c *could not* be nearly $170. by any possible calculation, so I suppose they must have charged some things for the whole year and it will not be so much the next half session. As to our uniforms Mrs. S. says it is *absolutely* necessary. She says there is but one shade of real tan color and I can get no pieces to send as sample but a right light shade would be prettier, I would like mine made with small tucks about a fingers width very high to the waist as you tuck muslin but if that is too troublesome please make a very wide hem nearly as wide as your arm from the elbow. Please make it over white cambric it will be much nicer. I want mine low necked with one of those long pointed capes, if they are worn now, trimmed with fringe of the same color, and long sleeves to take out with belts of the same color. Annie wants hers high necked but it will be too troublesome for you to have the bodies made, besides you can not fit us, Annie says she would rather have hers made here, and I think it would be best. Just send the trimming and belts. Please make my dress *long* and enough to turn under at the top as most of my dresses were deficient in that this winter. If necessary I can send a measure but I expect I am fully as tall as Sister and as the skirt will be sewed on to the dress here, it will not be necessary. Annie wants some chemises, and if you have seemstresses at leisure I should like two under skirts, but they are not absolutely necessary. Annie says please send her a pair of gaiters, and I want a pr also. My old ones have a hole or two in them, besides being generally worn out so they can only be worn in the house. Do not get them all around with *patent leather* it cracks all up. I have been very economical in shoes have only worn out one pr. since I have been here, and I brought very few with me. I would like my boots with heels I'll take good care of them and only wear them to church. Annie wants 4s I think, mine 2½, they will be full large. My last were twos they were rather broad but it would be bad to have them too small. Do you think I can do with my present every day dresses. I have my brown gingham and light chintz, that's all! Send my lawn skirt and I can wear it with one or two white bodies I have. Its body does not fit me so you need not send it. Do as you think about another dress. Annie is also thinking she wants another. Now please send me a collar a nice broad worked muslin to wear with my uniform dress. I have none except my lace one or the one trimmed with lace and the little one you sent me last fall which is rather narrow and thick to wear with summer clothes.

Then those two are really not enough. Annie says she would like one also. If you have a moderate sized piece of fine linen in the house won't you send it to me. I want to stitch a collar after a very pretty pattern the girls have here. And then a common fan, *not paper*. They tare so, and you know Grandpa did not give me one last summer. I have none—just a brown linen one with broad spokes to it. I have no doubt you have seen them often and it will last, and be most easily carried travelling. I do not think ruches are pretty without anything in them for our bonnets but then consult your taste. Do not think, dearest Mamma, we have many wants indeed I know if you could see my wardrobe you would agree with me, if you could hear a list of my other schoolmates wants you would think your daughters *very* moderate. Of course every Spring we all require new clothing and I am determined to do without as many things as I can. Mrs. S. says she does not want to have any bills here so it will be better to send everything from home. I am sorry this letter should be so filled but it is better to do it once and have it over. Send them as soon as you can. It will do no harm. Don't weary yourself unnecessarily. I am so glad you are going to Bath and do hope and pray you will be entirely recovered. I do long to see you well. As to the *hoops* I asked for certainly if you do not want to, don't send them. I don't care much for them. I merely thought it would be cooler in summer with very small ones. You must not, dear Mamma, compare our requirements with yours. You know you are confined very much to the house while we go about a good deal more need for bonnets and dresses and cloaks than you perhaps think. Mrs. S. gave, in her own parlor, a very nice little party (though it could scarcely be called one). Three young ladies and one young gentleman from town and about sixteen girls, Ada, Annette and myself included were present. Annie and Mary Stuart had headaches and Mary C did not wish to come down. It was very pleasant and nice refreshments. O I forgot please send me about 4 pr. of summer stockings, I have only thick winter ones and not many of them. You know I did not get but a single pr. last year and they are so large they fit Annie, besides they are winter stockings. I believe Annie is writing for what she wants. I will write soon again a more interesting letter and send Millie such a beautiful letter a little brother of one of my friends wrote his Mamma in Heaven. Write to us soon, dearest Mamma from your ever devoted daughter Agnes

I will again enumerate my "wants" as you always call them so you will have no trouble finding them when you want them. Bonnet, dress, worked collar, linen for an every day one, stockings 4 pr., gaiters, fan, underskirts and everyday dress if you think best. I'm afraid I can't do without the latter though I hope so. Much love to all. Please tell me Sister's direction. I would like to write to her.

Staunton Thursday 9th April '57

My precious Father,

I have something to tell you which I know will make you very happy. It is, I believe both of your daughters are Christians. I am sure Annie is, and O Papa I am resolved to doubt no longer that there has been a great and blessed change wrought in my wicked heart. That though I see now I am far more vile and desperately sinful than I ever had the smallest idea of, from this very knowledge I feel the insupportable weight of sin and the desire and the necessity of casting my burden at my Savior's feet and finding rest and peace where alone it can be found. I often feel a sweet peace stealing over me making me so very happy, calming my angry passions, & stilling my complaining tongue; a feeling of deep gratitude to my Father in Heaven who made me so wretched for some time to make me turn to Him, and to my Savior whose blessed promises of pardon and mercy to all who seek Him have raized me to hope and strive while before I was in dispair at the awfulness of my sins. At first the struggle was dreadful. We had been studying McIlvaine's "evidences of Christianity." Its beautiful style and interesting matter attracted me immediately. I did not then know, but soon found out, what momentous truths were most unquestionably proved it, and that he or she was worse than an idiot who could doubt the *reality* of religion. It set me to thinking, when I heard Bishop Johns was to confirm those disposed Easter. One Sunday when I had spent a most unprofitable day—at night I went into a room where two girls were weeping for their sins, then at once Mine stared me in the face in such awful magnitude—from that hour I had no rest. I wrote to Mamma she sent me a sweet comforting letter advising me to be confirmed if I had a single desire from henceforth to please God. Mr. Latane (our new minister) is a truly Christian man holiness is expressed in his very countenance he preaches true religion clearly and beautifully. His sermons have done me much good enlightened me on many dark points. I have been much blessed in every way. Mrs. Sheffey is *very* kind, personally interests herself in my (and every one's) advancement, and has done all in her power for me. I have conversed with Mr. Latane twice and like him very much. He told me yesterday he thought I might go up to the communion! I was *not* too young, and he did not think my great sense of unworthiness and sinfulness should prevent. I have not quite decided; the time is so near, and I fear so much I will dishonour His holy name, so my condemnation will be greater. But I feel sure I *earnestly* desire it, my tastes, my hopes, my pleasures, are very different from what they were, I have determined to lead a new life by *God's* help. The tempter puts so many dreadful thoughts in my mind which I have much difficulty in putting down. The first and oh! a powerful one was that I was so young—to put it off and enjoy myself until I had become weary of the pleasures of this world then it would be very well, but now it would make me deny myself so many anticipated gratifications, that Christians were so gloomy and so criticised *I* never could expect to pass as one in the estimation of others. Then he would make me believe my repentance was not sincere, that it was just an uneasy fancy which would leave me as before, so I must ask for no advice—tell no one. O these and numerous other temptations have beset me, dear Papa, and how can I thank God sufficiently that he has thus far kept me from falling back and has led me to strive on. I am sure I have always had your prayers and dear Mamma's. O I pity the human being who has never known a christian Father and Mother! Grandma sowed good seed in my young heart and often have her holy instructions come to me when I most needed them, O may her sainted spirit know how I thank her! I am left all alone in Mrs. Sheffey's sitting room. Bishop Johns arrived last Tuesday eve. Wed. morn. there was the consecration of our new church. Though my face was broken out with "roseola" I went. It was very beautiful and impressive, the more so, as I had never witnessed the ceremony before. And then the Bishop spoke so beautifully. He gave us a description of the Tabernacle or rather the Temple. We had just been studying about it in a book entitled the "Mine (Bible) explored." He explained each part but when he came to the Holy of Holies—the place of eternal rest, then indeed I realized the joy of the cause I have embraced and the glorious reward Christ awards to those who seek Him. But at night and this morning I could not go. It was a great disappointment this morning. Sadly I watched each passer to the house of God. Strangely must my tearful broken-out face have appeared as I gazed mournfully from the window, I know it was weak and wrong, now I feel contented, that it is a light trial to show me what very little patience and resignation I have.

Friday night.) I am again in Mrs. S.'s room to finish my letter to my own dear Papa. My face is much better but as the eruption has extended over my neck and arms, it burns and itches so I can't bear my bonnet strings under my throat. Yet I have not been deprived of all the services. O no, the rain so uncomfortable for others has exactly suited me, so last night and this morning our new school-room has made a capacious and suitable church. O Papa, I wish you could have heard his discourse (or extempore sermon last night. He described to us the agony in the garden, until I could almost imagine I was an eye witness of the scene. He told us of the cause of our Savior's dreadful sufferings. There He stood driving back the overwhelming wrath of an avenging God from a helpless guilty people! But my feeble pen is a mockery of his speaking language. Then he invited all to partake of the precious memorials of His body and blood. To pray that night for divine guidance, and to think He was saying to us *"By my agony and bloody sweat* take ye this &c, whether we meditated before closing our eyes for slumber or in the solemn hours of midnight to hear those same words. This morning his sermon was as beautiful, from "He has borne our griefs and carried our sorrows" All of his words went straight to my heart, and have done me much good. After service was over Mr. Phillips took me in to see him as before I was sick when he asked for me, and I had a very pleasant short conversation with him. He enquired very particularly after you. There are about fifteen girls to be confirmed, among them Mary, Ada, & Annette. We have all deep cause for thankfulness at the increased seriousness pervading this once frivolous school. Though I much fear it will soon pass away from the minds of many I feel sure there are some, may they not be few, where the Spirit has found an eternal abiding place. I have not yet thanked you for your last two letters, prized as usual. I am very grateful for your prompt long answers but, dear Papa, you must not deny yourself of needful slumber even though it deprive me of great pleasure but I can stand it better than you. I was so sorry to hear of Mr. Stockton's death. What has become of his poor wife? I am very happy for the pride you take in me, Papa, but alas it is far, far from being merited. I must stop or your eyes *will* be fatigued. I will write again soon. I have decided, dear Papa, to take the communion! Pray I may never dishonour the God I have taken? Yours ever

Agnes

I am sorry I made a mistake in the gender of the Good saint, as for the U.S. Army I used to believe it essential but something I heard I can't exactly remember how brought me to the conclusion it was not.

[Endorsed by R. E. Lee]
"My dear daughter Agnes narrating her struggles, doubts, final resolution, to give her heart to God & her life to his service"
Ans^d 11 May '57

Tuesday night—May 19th 1857
Your letter was received last night, dear Annie, so I hasten to answer it. I would have written Saturday though I had not heard from you, but we had a lesson to study in "Moral"—ten pages— and I had *so* much *mending* to do I found it was dinner time before I had completed. In the evening the "Sewing Society" took place with great success.

I am truly rejoiced you reached home safely though it seemed to me impossible for you to do otherwise *going home.* Mr. P. the morning after his return informed me of your safe arrival said you didn't have a bit of head-ache and that my "aunt's servant (Burke) most had a *fit* over Miss Anne." He said he *did* return to see you but was informed Ma. had come in for you and you had all gone home! But I must tell you of our proceedings from the time we parted at the depot—I not in the gayest mood as you might imagine. I had to say very often "only *six* weeks" to be contented with my fate. Agnes P. then took us [for] a nice ride—the fresh air made me feel much better. But our room looked sad and lonely and we all missed you very much. When left alone I knelt down and prayed dear Annie for your safe journey for the dear ones you would soon see & for contentment and submission which I think was granted me. Mary C. was for a time quite earnest in her protestations how she missed you & is still. She was excessively amused with Mr. Wheat the next morning, who after some hesitation, as he came to my name on the roll, came out with *"Miss Lee"* which he still continues. Mr. Engelbrecht said he was very sorry he did not see you that had he *known* you were going, he should have come over and told you goodbye, *at least.* (Excuse comme à l'ordinaire!) I teazed Mr. de Binzie sufficiently about your departure first telling him one thing then another until he concluded he wouldn't believe anything.

Friday eve. Mr. Latane came up to see us. After quietly waiting a half hour, th[r]ough some mistake of Mr. P's., we had quite a pleasant visit from him. He expressed regret at not seeing you. He has now gone away for some weeks. Harriette sends much love, she told me to put hers on a separate page, and tell you next time to send her *love alone.* Bettie received a letter from her little brother Gilmer. After waiting two or three *days* she opened it and found her father had not received one of her letters! Either her Aunt, or Willie Gatewood, I forget, sent her a very nice "box," part of its contents she sent to me which was *very nice.* I was just separating your portion according to custom, when lo! I found your place empty. Bettie has a dreadful sore throat. She can't speak above a whisper. Mr. & Mrs. P. have gone to the convention. Mr. P. will probably return Monday next. Mr. W. hears our lessons and very nicely. We have actually recited our first lesson in *"Butler"* it is only the *Introduction* but not very hard.

Last Friday we had our first exhibition rehearsal there was not much done. Mr. E. says I must play "Lucrezia Borzia." Nannie Argyle and I tried the duet Saturday. It went pretty well for the first time. Do tell us something about the comet? There is considerable excitement here, any no. of marvellous tales we would like to hear the truth. I think we will almost welcome its approach the weather is *so* cold. I almost regret sending my winter clothes home, fortunately my faithful red sack was left which is very comfortable. Is Mary Childe still with you, give *much* love to her and as many kisses as she sent me. Tell her I am just as anxious to

see her and will answer her *sweet* letter as soon as I hear where
she is by Her giving me her direction, "to *Baltimore*" I supposed
she would shortly return. Give also much love to Uncle Childe,
Cousin Florence, and Cousin Julia—and little Willie any no. of
kisses. It is too bad I can't see any of them! They must *all* wait
until I get *home*. Mary S. went into raphsodies over the part of
your letter saying Mr. P. was so kind and gentle. They both send
their best love, and say if *possible* will write Saturday. Any no. of
the girls send love. Bee. her best love and will write soon. Nannie
Smith also. She recieved tonight her long expected letter. Poor
girl! she was so agitated she could not open it & I had to perform
that operation. Her father has been very sick but is now much
better. I am so glad. Nellie sends much her "bessest" love & says to
tell you she tries very hard to keep Bee. and myself in order but
finds it a very hard task! Mary Bierne and several others send love.
& Mrs. Sheffey. I "reckon" you are tired of the word *love* but I give
O so much to *Mamma, Grandpa, Bob, Mill, & Cousin Markie*, with
my most affectionate remembrances to all the servants. O I can't
bear to think of you all so happy & I—far away. Indeed I think you
ought to come back, if you are well enough, which I sincerely
hope you very soon will be. My dress is finished it fits nicely. I will
send your trimmings in my next. there is not room now. I took a
long, but delightful walk to the woolen factory with Mr. W. the
evening of the day you left & was sufficiently tired on my return. I
have had several "compagnons de nuit" since your departure.
Bee. Scott is now as her room has no stove & we are obliged to
have fire all the time. Everything is very green but the weather
wintry. We actually had *snow* this morning early. Excuse this
terrible scratch. It is late & Butler claims my attention. You must
not imagine yourself *old and cold*; when you are well you will feel
very differently. I am so delighted *dear* Mamma is looking well. I
am not surprised at your liking Mary C. I am sure I will so much.

I send a letter from Laura to you. Mine has nearly the same in it.

She is probably at home now. Your letter was dated some *number-less* day in *March* how long was it coming I wonder! *Caroline* has just informed us she gives her *nicest* candlesticks to her favorites, and thereupon presented us with the two nicest in her basket. So you see we are not totally uncared for! You see you are "Staunton sick." You had much better never have left this charming spot—which really looks very pretty now. Write very soon & send me some flowers. Tell me how *everything* looks.

> With much love your
> devoted Sister
> Agnes

Annette sends her love—wants to be by *herself*.

AGNES' FAMILY
as mentioned in her Journal

George Washington Parke Custis (Grandpa) 1781–1857   m.   Mary Lee Fitzhugh (Grandma) 1788–1853

Mary Anne Randolph Custis (Mama) 1808–1873   m.   Robert Edward Lee* (Papa) 1807–1870

G. W. Custis Lee (Brother, Custis) 1832–1915

Wm. Henry Fitzhugh Lee (Fitzhugh, Fitz, Rooney) 1837–1891

Eleanor Agnes Lee (Agnes) author of journal 1841–1873

Mildred Childe Lee (Mil, Mildred) 1846–1905

Mary Custis Lee (Sister, Mary) 1835–1918

Anne Carter Lee (Annie) 1839–1862

Robert Edward Lee, Jr. (Rob) 1843–1914

*Robert Edward Lee was the son of Henry Lee ("Light Horse Harry," 1756–1818) and Anne Hill Carter (1773–1829).

Index